ARTFUL
SPACES

First published in the United States of America by North Light Books,
an imprint of F+W Media, Inc., 4700 East Galbraith Road, Cincinnati, Ohio 45236
800-289-0963

First published in Australia in 2008 by Murdoch Books, Pier 8/9, 23 Hickson Road,
Millers Point NSW 2000, Australia, a division of Murdoch Books Pty Limited.

Chief Executive: Juliet Rogers
Publishing Director: Kay Scarlett

Project manager and editor: Paul O'Beirne
Design concept and designer: Alex Frampton
Photographer: Alan Benson
Production: Nikla Martin

ISBN-13: 978-1-60061-459-0
ISBN-10: 1-60061-459-0

Color separation by Splitting Image in Clayton, Victoria, Australia.
Printed by i-Book Printing Ltd. in 2008. PRINTED IN CHINA.

The products photographed in this book have been used as examples for photography only
and are not endorsed by Murdoch Books, nor is Murdoch Books sponsored by these
companies in any way.

ARTFUL
SPACES

DIY wall art for the home

GERARD SMITH

North Light Books
Cincinnati, Ohio
www.artistsnetwork.com

Contents

CHAPTER FOUR

CLEANING UP: IT'S A PAIN, BUT SOMEONE'S GOT TO DO IT

CHAPTER FIVE

AND ONTO THE PROJECTS ...

CHAPTER SIX

INSPIRATION

CHAPTER SEVEN

MASKED, MAN

CHAPTER EIGHT

MEDIUMS WELL DONE

CHAPTER NINE

COLLAGE

Thanks Dave, for giving me the job in the first place.

PROJECT GALLERY

pg 138

pg 110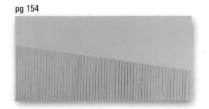

pg 58

pg 54

pg 158

pg 186

pg 150

pg 154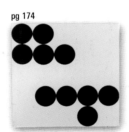

pg 106

pg 194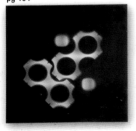

pg 174

pg 92

pg 162

pg 88

pg 102

126

pg 62

pg 130

pg 190

pg 80

pg 178

pg 134

pg 182

pg 84

Introduction

I don't see riches, I don't see love, but I do see a lot of paint ...

I suppose I should say at the outset that I'd hit rock bottom and art saved my life, but I'd be lying if I did. No, my involvement with art happened slowly and much less dramatically. I liked coloring books as a child and was good at art in school, but I don't seriously think anyone responds with 'art store retail assistant' when asked 'What do you want to do, when you grow up?'. I certainly didn't. I was going to be a bank manager, married to Samantha Fox.

After I'd finished a social science degree, I moved to Sydney and started working in a series of jobs that were never quite me. So I began to do other things on the side. I made lino prints and sold them to gift stores, and helped a couple of guys make picture frames to sell at Paddington Markets.

I eventually ended up doing system-administration work for a large computer company. I wasn't crazy about the job, but the people I worked with were a great bunch. So I continued to work there and did my creative things on the side. My prints morphed into a range of cards that took off commercially, and I started to paint in acrylics. Things were looking good. Then one day, another department at work offered me a job. There was a huge pay increase involved, so I took the bait. From the first day I knew it was a bad move. I absolutely hated it and was canned six months later. It was then I decided to study graphic design full time. I figured that if I was going to do creative work then I should make a career out of it. But I would need a casual job to help pay the bills. So when I walked past my local art store and saw a 'help wanted' sign in the window I made an appointment and found myself working there the following Saturday.

At first I was unsure. What did all these products do? Who bought them? And what did I have to do to get the naked alcoholic homeless man out of the store? So, I started to read art-technique books, try products and go to evening-college courses. I became a graphic designer, but liked the art store so much I didn't really want to leave. Eventually, I decided to do both jobs part time. And I still do.

(By the way, if you ever need to get a naked alcoholic homeless man out of a store, wave some money at him and lure him outside. Once outside, give him the money and shut the door until he wanders off. Works every time.)

THE WEEKEND ARTIST AND WHAT IT MEANS

I've been working in an east Sydney art store for a few years now, and I've recently noticed a change in our clientele. Not long ago, it was all hard-core artists and shoplifting drug addicts (not forgetting the nude alcoholic homeless types.) But now we also attract a different type of customer. This new breed of artist wants to live in apartments with dishwashers, instead of garrets with vermin. They want a regular income instead of regular debt. They are into clean lines, but want to live above the poverty line. They work 9–5 but are free on the weekends to do whatever they want. And what they want to do is something creative.

I call these types weekend artists.

Many people assume the artistic world and the rest of the working world do not mix, but that simply isn't the case. Very few young artists can make a living from their art alone, which accounts for the rudeness of approximately 60 per cent of Sydney's service industries. I also believe there is a strong desire for people to express themselves artistically without taking a vow of poverty. After all, Sydney is an expensive town.

I've often helped budding weekend-artist types. They know they want to do a painting, but don't really know where to begin. We would often get talking and I would sketch up a few ideas and give them a few tips. I have to say it's enormously satisfying when customers bring back photographs of their work to show me. One guy even brought his painting into the store (although he wouldn't show it to me until we were in a quiet area of the store). I could tell he was impressed with what he'd done. And I was too.

So, what I've tried to do is assemble information based on the questions I hear week-in-week-out. I've also tried to come up with projects that actually look good. I was so sick of seeing dreadful projects on television and in magazines. Does anyone really want to make something out of seashells, glue and a few pieces of rope stuck onto a board? They've got to be kidding, but I suspect they're not. I wouldn't want something like that on my wall and I don't think you do either. I also understand that weekend artists want something that is reasonably quick, so I've included projects that take hardly any time at all, some that take a little bit more time and others that take a bit more time still.

So, if you've got 48 spare hours, then I've got the project for you. There will be no seashells involved, I promise.

Acrylic paints

"Do you need any help there or are you just looking?"

Painting is a bit like picking your nose; you did a lot of it when you were at school but you haven't done much of it since. And if you have, you certainly don't do it as freely as you did as a child. So, what usually drives people to go back to the brush?

Sooner or later, most people move out of home or leave share accommodation and finally get a place they want to call home. Then one day, when all the furniture is in place and the earthenware's unpacked, they stand in the middle of the new space and think 'I need something for that empty wall'. So they start to look at a few galleries and think to themselves: 'I could do better than that!' or 'They're charging how much?!'

And that's how they usually end up talking to me in the art store.

I can spot them a mile away. They wander around the store looking slightly lost. I usually approach them and the conversation goes something like this:

Me: Do you need any help?

Customer: Yeeeeeah. I just feel like doing a bit of painting.

Me: Have you painted before?

Customer: At school.

Me: So are you after oil paints or acrylics?

Customer: What's the difference?

This reply tells me that I am indeed in the presence of an amateur, which then also means that it's time for me to give a quick lesson on the Joy of Acrylic Paints. Most people have used acrylic paints at school. Acrylics tend to have a reputation for being the poor relation to oil paints, probably because they were only invented in the 1930s and don't have that grand historic oil painting thing going on. It may also be down to the fact that their high school art room had only approximately four containers of the cheapest acrylic paint in the world, shared between 35 students. And an art teacher who doubled

The **INFORMATION** in these two chapters will form the basis for projects in later sections, so sit up straight and **PAY ATTENTION**. Especially you in the back row.

as a careers advisor, yet knew next to nothing about art. The one thing that teacher did know, with absolute certainty, is that becoming an artist is the worst career decision you could ever make. Or maybe that's just me.

Anyway, I always try to steer people in the direction of acrylic paints. It's the way to go for all you weekend artists out there. So forget those bad art room experiences. Both your hairstyle and acrylic paints have changed since then.

JUST WHAT ARE ACRYLIC PAINTS?

Basically, acrylic paints are pigments suspended in an acrylic polymer emulsion. They dry to a semi-matte plastic finish. Well, that's enough exciting technical information for today.

DO I USE THEM STRAIGHT FROM THE TUBE/POT? DO I NEED TO ADD WATER OR SOMETHING?

Nope, you don't need to add anything to acrylic paints—maybe just a little water if the paint's too thick. Basically you just dip that brush in, then start slappin'.

THERE'S LOTS OF BRANDS AND PRICES. CAN I MIX THEM TOGETHER?

You certainly can. The basic formula of practically all acrylic paints is very similar, so there should be no problems at all. Don't ever feel that all your paints have to come from one brand.

MOMMY, WHERE DO ACRYLIC PAINTS COME FROM?

Acrylic paints in their current form have only been around since the 1950s, although their beginnings can be traced back to Mexico in the early 1930s. Around 1947, the world's first artist acrylic paints, known as Magna, were developed by Sam Golden while he was working for his uncle Leonard Bocour of Bocour Artist Colors. These paints had a strong spirit base and were considerably more toxic than the products we have today. Acrylics certainly are the toddlers of the art world when you consider that oil paints can be traced back as far as the eight century. In 1955, the first water-based acrylic paint, called Liquitex, was developed by a company called Permanent Pigments—and they're still available today, God bless 'em!

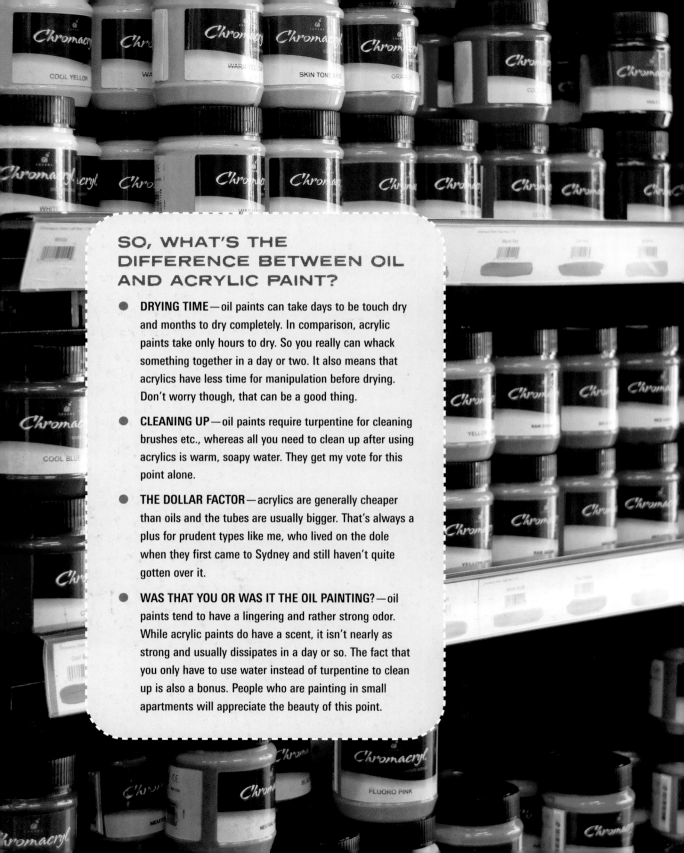

SO, WHAT'S THE DIFFERENCE BETWEEN OIL AND ACRYLIC PAINT?

- **DRYING TIME**—oil paints can take days to be touch dry and months to dry completely. In comparison, acrylic paints take only hours to dry. So you really can whack something together in a day or two. It also means that acrylics have less time for manipulation before drying. Don't worry though, that can be a good thing.

- **CLEANING UP**—oil paints require turpentine for cleaning brushes etc., whereas all you need to clean up after using acrylics is warm, soapy water. They get my vote for this point alone.

- **THE DOLLAR FACTOR**—acrylics are generally cheaper than oils and the tubes are usually bigger. That's always a plus for prudent types like me, who lived on the dole when they first came to Sydney and still haven't quite gotten over it.

- **WAS THAT YOU OR WAS IT THE OIL PAINTING?**—oil paints tend to have a lingering and rather strong odor. While acrylic paints do have a scent, it isn't nearly as strong and usually dissipates in a day or so. The fact that you only have to use water instead of turpentine to clean up is also a bonus. People who are painting in small apartments will appreciate the beauty of this point.

HOW TO READ A TUBE OF ACRYLIC PAINT

Even though I've worked in an art store for years, I have to confess that I still don't quite know what all the information on a tube of acrylic paint means. So, like I always say, when in doubt ask a sales rep! Even if they don't know the answer, someone back at Acrylic-Paint Headquarters will (and in this case they did).

Color sample

Not all tubes have this, but most will have some sort of color indicator on the tube. Other brands may have a printed swatch that is not a completely accurate representation of the paint's color. There may be some sample boards available. But whatever you do, don't be one of those customers who opens the tube and smears a sample on the stand. That's really annoying.

Quality description

This indicates that a tube of paint is artist quality, as opposed to student quality.

Series number

You will often find that artist-quality acrylics have a Series number. Basically, the higher the number, the higher the price, because the pigment required for a higher Series number is more expensive.

Star rating for permanence

This permanency rating indicates how stable the color will remain. With the exception of fluorescent colors, which lose their luminous qualities in a few weeks, the majority of artist-quality acrylics have excellent permanency. This color is no exception. Four stars = excellent permanency.

TRANSPARENCY

Acrylic paints are not all the same in terms of their opacity. You may also see markings on tubes indicating their transparency levels. Although there is no standard coding for this, I have thrown together a small table that shows the meaning of symbols and letters that I have seen on various tubes.

SYMBOL	LETTER	OPACITY LEVEL
○	T	Transparent
◑	SO	Semi Opaque
●	O	Opaque

If a paint is marked as transparent, there really is no way to make it opaque. The only thing you can do is apply successive coats to build up the color. On the other hand, you can make an opaque paint more transparent by adding a medium or two. (I go into this in more detail in Chapter 8, so turn there now if the suspense is killing you.)

WHAT'S UP WITH HUE?

You may notice that some acrylic paints have the word 'hue' after their name. As the color of acrylic paints is derived from particular pigments, hue is simply a blend of pigments that are designed to look like the genuine color. For example, a tube marked Cadmium Red has real ground cadmium pigment, but a tube labeled Cadmium Red Hue contains a blend of cheaper, non-cadmium pigments and dyes that mimic the real color. Hue colors exist because the real pigment may be too expensive, unavailable or even toxic.

STUDENTS VS. ARTISTS

When shopping for acrylic paints, you may find that you have to choose between 'artist' and 'student' quality. Artist-quality paint is generally formulated with real pigment, and the price varies with the expense of the pigment. Paints are often graded in terms of 'Series', with levels from 1–4 (4 being the most expensive). In comparison, student-quality paints have synthetic pigments and a limited range of colors. They are not graded by Series, and the texture can be thinner. I've also noticed that the color isn't quite as strong, which may mean that you need to apply successive coats to get the color intensity you're after. If you're starting out, pick a selection of both so you can see the difference for yourself.

ARE THE PAINTS YOU BUY IN AN ART STORE THE SAME AS HOUSEHOLD ACRYLIC PAINTS?

Yes and no. The base formulas are the same and they have similar qualities in terms of rapid drying and cleaning up, but the main differences are in the texture and pigment. Household paints are much thinner so they can be used to cover a large surface quickly. Consequently, they are also prone to run and drip. Artists' paints are thicker and contain real pigment, giving them much greater color permanency. However, the big advantage of house paints is that they come in a huge variety of colors, and the nice person in the paint store can practically match any color you bring in with you.

SO, CAN I USE THEM OR WHAT?

Yes you can. You'll find that I use them frequently in my projects, but only when I don't want any texture at all. For example, you can use them to paint a canvas flat beige before adding textured sections with artist acrylic paints. You'll also have to go to a hardware store or decorating center to buy tester pots because they're not sold in art stores. The one warning I would give you is to keep an eye out for any pesky drips running down the side of your canvas.

SPOT THE STUDENT

This is an example of a tube of student acrylic. As you can see, not only does it say that it is a student acrylic (I know it's obvious, but I do like to point these things out), it also has no Series number or star rating for permanence as opposed to the fancy-pants artist tube on page 19.

2

What colors should I use?

Picking colors can be more difficult than you would imagine. Most customers I speak to can tell me their favorite color, but it's another story when it comes to naming a favored color combination. So how do you know what colors you like in the first place?

HOW TO PICK COLORS

- Find an example of a painting you like. What colors are used in the painting?
- Look at your clothes. Most people have certain colors that they wear together and are comfortable with.
- Again, look at your furniture. What are the predominant colors?
- Natural landscapes and objects are often perfectly color coordinated. You never hear anyone look at a rose and say 'that pink looks terrible with that green'. Mother Nature knows her cookies when it comes to putting combinations together. Steal her ideas—it's not as if she can sue.

If all else fails, go for the Art Store Guy's 3-Color Rule.

THE ART STORE GUY'S 3-COLOR RULE

Pick one color and a shade of that color; then, add another color of your choice. Stick to just three colors and you have a good chance of creating a painting that doesn't look like a dog's breakfast, or more to the point, what the dog does after breakfast. There's nothing scientific or intellectual about this concept, it's just something I've noticed that tends to work quite well.

The other thing you can do is use black and white and another single color of your choice. That always looks pretty good too.

Here are some examples to show you what I mean.

Examples

Directly below is a project from Chapter 7 that uses the 3-color rule. To the right are two other examples, showing other possible color combinations that could also be used. The beauty of the 3-color rule is that it offers quite a range of color combinations that look good together—even the most picky weekend artist will find a combination that they like.

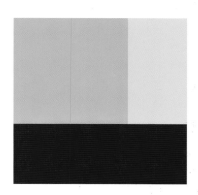

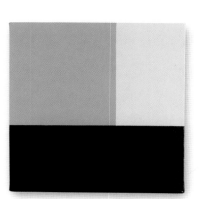

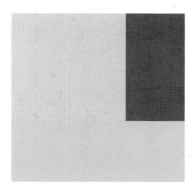

THE DARK SIDE OF ACRYLICS

What you see initially isn't what you get. Bear in mind that all acrylic paints dry about 15–20 percent darker than when you first paint them on, so wait until the paint dries before you start judging a book by its color.

WHAT + WHAT = WHAT?

I'm almost embarrassed to admit this, but I've never felt all that comfortable with a color wheel. It's just too mathematical for me. In fact, the one I have is now busy gathering dust in my garage. Although there's a wealth of information in that one pretty wheel, I'm sure there must be others like me who just want to know what they have to mix with what in order to get what. Well, for all those color wheel challenged types I hope this helps. (If not, just give up and buy pre-mixed colors. I personally think this is the best way to go when you're first starting to paint.)

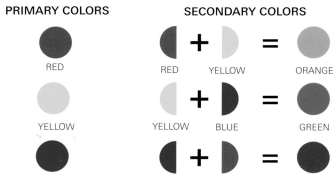

PRIMARY COLORS

RED

YELLOW

BLUE

SECONDARY COLORS

RED + YELLOW = ORANGE

YELLOW + BLUE = GREEN

BLUE + RED = VIOLET

TERTIARY COLORS

RED + ORANGE = RED ORANGE

YELLOW + GREEN = YELLOW GREEN

BLUE + VIOLET = BLUE VIOLET

RED + VIOLET = RED VIOLET

YELLOW + ORANGE = YELLOW ORANGE

BLUE + GREEN = BLUE GREEN

Primary colors
are the Adams & Eves of the art world because they can't be made from other colors.

Secondary colors
are the kids of the primarys. Two primarys equals one secondary.

Tertiary
Maybe I should have lain off the family analogies because tertiary colors are the results of one primary and one secondary. Things are gettin' creepy round here!

a **TINT** is a color + white   a **TONE** is a color + gray   a **SHADE** is a color + black

MIXMASTER

Although I think you should start off with pre-mixed colors, there is going to come a day when you want to make your own. So for all you mixing mavericks out there, here's a few pointers:

- **Mix colors with a spare brush, not the one you're using**—although it's tempting to use the brush you're painting with, it's not a good idea. Not only do you end up with a brush thickly covered in paint, you also get streaking of colors on the canvas because some of the unmixed colors inevitably cling to your brush. Try and keep a cheap brush on the side just for mixing. You can always use plastic spoons or something similar for the same purpose.

- **Add a dark color to a lighter color**—it is much easier to control the mixing this way, which leads me to my next point.

- **Take it slowly**—while it is tempting to just squirt out a whole lotta paint, you run the risk of going way beyond the desired color. Then you have to add more of the opposing color and before you know it you've used up a tube of paint and all you've got is a big blob of a mixed color that isn't quite right. So take it slowly. Remember, first we crawl, then we walk, then we walk to the pub and crawl home. Or something like that.

What else do I need?

So now that the brief acrylic lesson is over, it's time to move on to all the other things you might need to get your weekend-artist career up and running.

BRUSHES

I always like to start with the brush section. There really is something quite charming about rows of different brushes standing to attention. It's also rather intimidating if you don't know what's what. So let's start with basic brush anatomy ...

Brush Bits

You may have noticed that some brushes are long handled and some are short handled. The shorter brushes are generally for smaller scale work and details—they allow greater control of the bristles. As you might expect, longer brushes are for larger canvases—makes sense when you stop and think about it.

Most brushes also have a number. This indicates the size of bristles/brush. The higher the number the larger the size of the bristles/brush. See, this one's a No. 8.

Bristle
The bristles are just that, although they can be either natural or synthetic. They are generally attached to the rest of the brush with glue.

Handle
It's not just a handle. It usually displays the brand and the size of the brush, and hopefully a description of the bristle.

Ferrule
The metal part of the brush that determines the shape of the bristles, be they flat or round.

THE USUAL BRUSH SPECS

Although I specify in each project which brushes I use, I thought it would be a good idea to go over some brush styles and their uses. And I get to use one of my corny puns. Hooray! These are typically the types of brushes you'll see in most art stores. There are more, but I don't think we need to get too carried away.

Flat

My personal favorite, the flat brush, is basically good for filling in large areas. They are also useful for blending but not as smoothly as the fan brush.

Round

When people think of brushes, they're thinking of this one. These are good for lines and strokes, not so great for filling in large surface areas.

Fan

I used to see these in the store and not really know what they were about. They are primarily for blending colors that are side by side. Because the bristles are less densely packed than other brushes the result is a very smooth graduation of color. They really do a remarkable job.

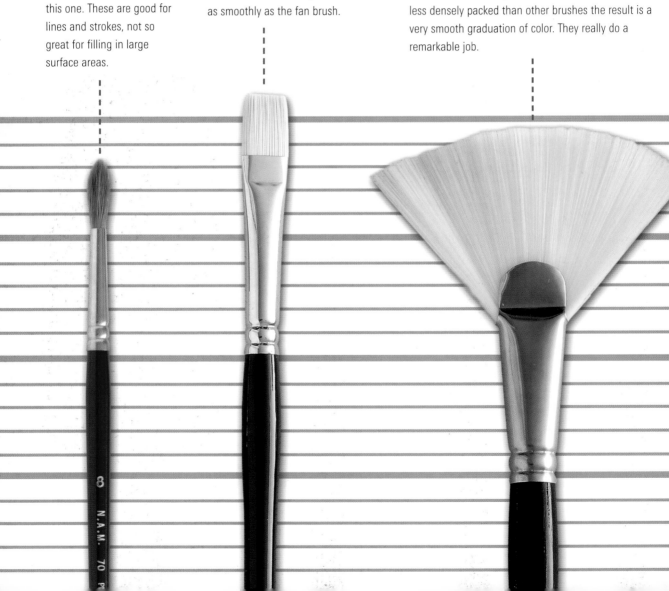

Filbert

These are like a cross between a round and a flat brush. Their flat shape and slightly rounded sides are useful for softening edges.

Brights

Brights are like flat brushes after they've had a haircut and settled down. With their short, flat bristles they are good for details and can leave more texture.

Rigger

These long, thin brushes are really only good for painting long, thin lines. Funny that.

House

Yes, you can use the good old garden-variety house-painting brushes that you find in hardware stores. As you might expect, they hold a lot of paint and are useful for covering large, flat surfaces. They're like the chubbier cousin of the flat brush, although everyone makes an effort not to comment on their size at family gatherings.

LICK MY LOLLY...

NOT THE BRUSHES

ROUND
Versatile brush,
excellent for fine &
delicate strokes, broad
strokes & flat washes

SPITTING TIPS

We have a sign in the store requesting that customers refrain from licking the brushes. It seems odd, but people do it to determine the type of tip the bristles make. Not only is it pretty gross to see, but I have also been told that brushes are sprayed with some chemical to get them through customs. I don't know if that's an urban myth or not, but it's probably best to keep them out of your mouth. If you must check the tip with spit (shame on you!) then at least spit on your finger first and then apply it to the brush.

And don't forget, you never know which part of the badger, sable or hog those bristles came from!

NATURAL VS. SYNTHETIC

The good news is that natural and synthetic brushes are both suitable for acrylic painting, so take your pick. Bear in mind that rougher brushes, such as hog hair, tend to give more texture whereas finer smooth-hair brushes, such as synthetics, result in a smoother more even surface. Synthetic bristles are also somewhat less flexible than their natural counterparts. As for price, I've found cheaper brushes tend to lose more hair, which can be annoying. My advice: start cheap (either natural or synthetic) and if you get into it start to add a few more pricier brushes to see what works for you.

WAITER, THERE'S A HAIR IN MY PAINTING ...

There really is no easy solution to this one. Sometimes the brush you're using will leave heaps of annoying hairs in your painting. To offset this you can wash your brush before you use it and pull at the bristles in order to remove any loose hairs, but other than that you'll just have to keep using the brush until the shedding subsides or try another one. Sigh.

I have found that it is easier to remove hairs from wet paint with a cloth wrapped around your finger. Just dab at the hair until it comes away. It's a lot cleaner and more efficient than scratching away with your fingernail or using two bare fingers to pick it off. Failing that, I also try to pick the offending hair up with my brush before wiping it off on a spare piece of newspaper.

WANT TO RUIN YOUR BRUSHES NOW? ASK ME HOW!

The quickest way to wreck almost any brush is to leave it overnight, bristles down, in a jar of water. I know you think you'll clean it up the next day, but by then the damage will be done. The bristles will almost certainly be splayed out at some crazy angle, never to return to their old pointed selves ever again. In addition, all that soaking can affect the glue in the brush, so even if you do use the brush again the hairs will come out all over the place and the actual brush itself might even come apart. It really is worth taking those extra few minutes to clean brushes properly and save yourself an unnecessary trip back to the art store.

THINK OUTSIDE
THE PALETTE

Palettes are usually thin boards on which artists mix paints. Most people will think of a palette as one of those kidney-shaped things with a hole in it. The artist balances the palette with his thumb through the hole and mixes a rich tapestry of colors to best represent the Rubenesque beauty posing in front of him. Before long, artist and model are writhing on the floor as candlelight dances upon their naked flesh.

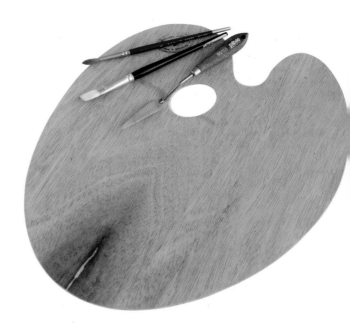

Now, where was I? That's right, I was going on about palettes. Anyway, not all palettes have this romantic image. My favorite palettes were previously used as containers for my local Indian butter chicken special, and I can assure you there's nothing romantic about that. Yes, if you haven't already guessed, takeout containers (and their lids) are my palettes of choice. But don't assume you have to wait until you don't feel like cooking, because practically any jar, lid or plastic container can be used as a palette.

If you do decide to buy a commercial palette don't go for the flat, kidney-shaped artistic-looking ones, unless you are doing a smallish painting. There just isn't a lot of room on them, and novice painters tend to get a bit excited and use a lot of paint. Buy one that looks like a plastic muffin tin, as they keep the paint in the wells and allow you to squeeze or mix larger quantities of paint without the colors accidentally moving in together. I mean, what would their parents think?

Another option is the disposable palette. This is usually a pad of tear-off, coated paper that you use and then throw away. I'm not some mad greenie but it does seem a bit wasteful. However, they do come in handy if you're painting outdoors or just couldn't be bothered cleaning up. A far cheaper alternative is to use an old magazine—just use the pages to mix paint on. When you need to use another color you can simply turn the page and start again. The one disadvantage of this is that the pages aren't plain white, so you may find yourself squeezing magenta acrylic all over Paris Hilton's face or mixing colors on Courtney Love's latest plastic surgery horror. Still, that could be oddly satisfying in itself.

PALETTE POINTERS

- Acrylic paints dry quickly, so don't go crazy and squeeze out the entire contents of the tube onto the palette. Just squeeze out a bit at a time and top up as needed.

- If you live in a particularly dry climate, you may need to keep a water mister handy to lightly mist your paint—this will stop it drying out too quickly. I've never had to do this, but I am told it works quite well.

- Plastic wrap can be used to seal the paint on your palette if you take a long break. It will stop it from drying out.

EASEL DODGERS TIP

If you do all your painting on a newspaper-covered table, you may find that when you paint the side of the pre-stretched canvas it can stick to the newspaper and you'll have to have one almighty ripping session to get the two apart after the paint dries. While it's not something to talk to your doctor about, it can be avoided by placing a takeout container lid (or something like it) at one end so only one side of the canvas touches the newspaper. Then, when the whole thing dries you only have to remove newspaper from one side. I've done this with practically every project in this book, so this advice comes from the Voice of Experience.

EASELS: DO I NEED ONE?

Almost every project in this book was done on my kitchen table. However, the main drawback of working on a table is that you are painting on a horizontal surface (so you may have to lean over your artwork, which will distort your perspective of any larger artworks you work on); whereas with an easel you are painting on a vertical surface, which doesn't distort your perspective. You can also use an easel to display your finished work, so it can double as a stand. But it's really not an absolute necessity. If you're going to do a few one-off projects you don't really need an easel. Your table will do just fine. Just don't tell my manager I said that.

PALETTE KNIVES

Palette knives are those small trowel-like things that are primarily used for paint mixing. I always thought they were a bit of a waste of time until I used one. They really are extremely good for adding small amounts of paint to another color for mixing. But the palette knife isn't all about mixing; they are also used for painting and adding texture to paint on the canvas.

Their versatility really does make them worth owning—but buy a cheap plastic one if you must. If you go for a metal one be sure to wipe it dry after washing. Mine always seem to go rusty if I don't.

OTHER IMPLEMENTS

As you flick through my projects you'll notice that I try to incorporate everyday items into making my work. The lesson to learn here is that you don't necessarily need specialized equipment. So next time you're near a second-hand store or bargain store drop in and look for unusually shaped kitchen implements. Would this bottle make a good stamp? Could that mixing tool leave an interesting mark if pressed into wet paint? Perhaps that plastic thing could be used to drag paint across a canvas.

Don't be afraid to experiment with various objects. If it doesn't work, keep going until you find something that does. There's a lot of options out there, so keep your peepers peepin'!

WATER-BASED GLOSS VARNISH

I use this extensively in my paintings. Basically, it's a water-based varnish that adds a glossy finish to your final paintings. Big deal I hear you say. Well it is a big deal, because it makes a big difference to the depth of your colors and the overall finish of your work. One of the common complaints about acrylic paints is that they dry to a matte finish that lacks color depth. This is where gloss varnish comes to the rescue. You'll need about two coats minimum to get a good shine, and even though it's a milky color in the container it dries clear. The difference it makes is remarkable. It can even give acrylic painting a similar finish to oil painting.

I don't want to confuse you but this little beauty can also be mixed with acrylic paints for a colored transparent glaze-like finish. Varnishes also come in satin and matte, but the gloss version remains a staple in my projects, although I do use the others as well. Oh yeah, and because it's water based you clean up with water, just like regular acrylics.

CAUTION—Don't brush gloss varnish excessively! If you keep brushing as it starts to dry, the varnish will 'ball' and dry to a patchy white color. Yucko! Just slap it on quickly and leave it alone to dry before going in for that second coat.

PRE-STRETCHED CANVAS

Pre-stretched canvases really are sex on a stick to the weekend artist. They are readily available in a range of sizes and prices, and look great unframed on a wall. What more could you ask for—except maybe sex on a stick? I thought I'd give you a quick rundown on the most common questions I hear about them.

WHAT'S THE DIFFERENCE BETWEEN A PRE-STRETCHED CANVAS AND ONE I MAKE MYSELF?

Pre-stretched canvases usually have a lightweight wooden frame and the canvas is thinner. If you make one yourself you can customize the size to whatever you're after, whereas pre-stretched canvases come in standard sizes. You can also pick the sort of canvas you prefer to use.

While pre-stretched canvases have a lightweight frame, the frames you make yourself from individual stretcher bars (they're the wooden pieces that make up the frame) are sturdier. But don't let these differences put you off pre-stretched canvases. They're perfect for what we're trying to accomplish here.

CAN I PAINT STRAIGHT ON IT?

Canvas needs to be primed with what's called a gesso in order to seal it and give the paint something to adhere to. The good news is that I've yet to find a pre-stretched canvas that isn't already primed. However, if you want to check for yourself, just compare the color of the canvas on the front to the color on the back. If the front color is noticeably white, it has most likely been

I HAD AN OLD SHOEBOX HERE SOMEWHERE ...

When you start to buy a few art supplies you will no doubt want to store them in something. An old cardboard shoebox is a good place to start, but there are other options you may want to consider. Art stores sell a variety of boxes that look like wooden briefcases with little compartments inside. If you are buying a gift for the oil painter in your life and want maximum wow factor, these cases are the way to go. However, for sheer practicality go to your nearest hardware store and buy a sturdy toolbox—that's if your art store doesn't stock them, of course! They come in a range of sizes and are roomy enough for you to throw everything into after you've finished. Some even have shallow trays that are good for brushes, pencils, scissors and any other little bits and pieces. They are also quite lightweight and it doesn't matter if the inside gets all messy with paint. In fact, I think that adds to their charm.

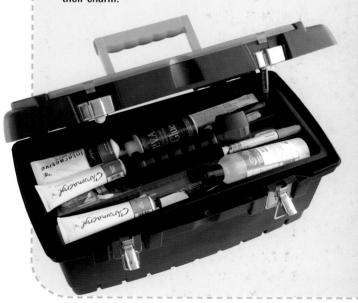

Would You Like Wedges With That?

When you buy a pre-stretched canvas you often get a small pack of eight little wooden (or plastic) triangles on the back. These are called wedges and are used to prevent the stretchers from bowing. They also help keep the canvas taut. You simply use a hammer to tap them into the slots (thinnest point first) where the frames meet. No glue is needed. There are two wedges per corner, so wedge loneliness isn't a problem. I personally only use them on larger canvases because they are more likely to bow than the little bitty ones.

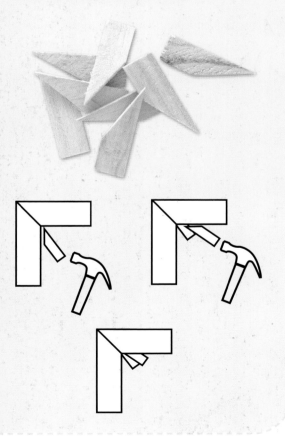

primed. The canvas on the back is usually unprimed and will be cream/light brown in color.

IS IT CHEAPER TO STRETCH MY OWN CANVAS?

Generally not. In order to do your own canvas you will need a range of equipment, including stretcher bars, a mallet, a set square, canvas, a staple gun, staples, a staple remover, a hammer and stretching pliers. In addition, you'll have to know what you are doing and that only comes with practice. So my advice is to start off with the pre-stretched canvas and if you decide to do your own, find someone to show you how. Community colleges and art schools sometimes run workshops on this. You can read about how to do it, but I personally think finding a good teacher is the best way to go.

SHOULD I GET THE THICK OR THE THIN ONES?

Most places sell pre-stretched canvases that range from about ½" to 1½" in depth. I say go for the thickest as there really isn't that much difference in price and they do look much better on a wall. Having said that, it's no big deal if you have to use the thin ones. One thing you should look out for is staples on the side of the canvas. Ideally, the staples should be on the back of the frame. It's not the end of the world but a clean edge looks better. This is an easy thing to overlook. In fact, I'm adding this point because I made this very mistake yesterday and really couldn't be bothered taking it back to do an exchange. It's going to become my experimental canvas.

I DON'T LIVE NEAR AN ART STORE

Other avenues for sourcing art supplies

I'm from the country myself so I can really relate to this one. And although you may not have an art store close by, you probably do have some art supplies available locally. You just have to know where to look.

BARGAIN STORES—I traveled around the country last year and was surprised to find that practically every small town had one of these stores. You know the type, crammed full of everything, with plastic storage bins and a junk jewelry stand out the front. Look inside and you almost always find a section with some art supplies, particularly brushes and pre-stretched canvases. There are also acrylic paints, and although the quality isn't going to set new standards, sometimes you just have to make do with what you can get.

HARDWARE STORES—Good for brushes, adhesives and things that you need to hang your painting. You can also buy sample pots of acrylic paints that you can use for paintings that don't require any texture.

NEWSSTANDS—You can buy papers for collage and sketchpads. Markers and pencils are also available.

LARGE CHAIN STORES—Target and Kmart are all over the country and they often have a small section with paints, brushes and pre-stretched canvases. They usually stick it somewhere near the toy section. Also, have a look for collage papers in their stationery areas.

SUPERMARKETS—You can buy adhesives, permanent markers and wrapping papers suitable for collage. Sometimes they have paints and brushes near the stationery and these are worth checking out.

BOOK LIQUIDATION STORES—I always like wandering around these temporary stores in search of something to read. I've noticed that quite a few of these stores have a small range of art materials as well. No guarantees here as far as quality goes but worth a look anyway.

STATIONERY STORES—These have all manner of papers for collage, basics like scissors and pencils, and a wide selection of markers, which is good news if you've decided to take the street-art route.

THE INTERNET—Whatever did we do before the internet? You can make internet purchases and browse art stores and company sites online to find out more. Don't forget eBay. You'll be surprised what's available for auction. Or disappointed with what's not. One of the two!

DO I NEED TO FRAME IT?

God no. In fact, pre-stretched canvases look better if you don't frame them. Just look in almost any art gallery and you'll see a lot of frameless paintings. All you have to do is hang it directly on the wall. (See Chapter 12 for more on how to hang your paintings.)

ONE STRETCHED CANVAS, HANGIN' ON THE WALL

There are two other things you need to consider when you're buying stretched canvases. These are size and quantity. Customers frequently tell me they've got a blank wall they want to fill and then want to know the size of the biggest canvas we've got. Although you may have a huge blank wall you don't necessarily need the mother of all stretched canvases to fill it. Why not try two, three or even four smaller ones?

Don't forget that you can also combine different-sized canvases. And don't feel that oblongs and squares can't be mixed. I could rave on all day about the options, but that would bore both of us to death. Just have a gawk at the following examples. I think you'll see what I mean.

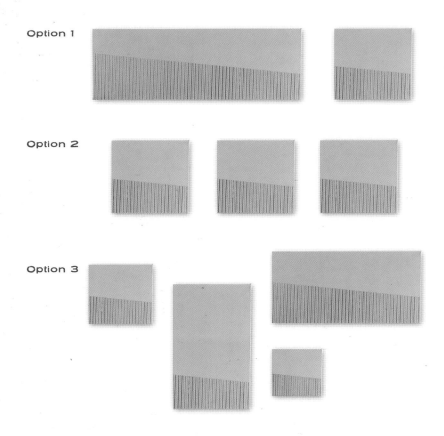

Cleaning up:

it's a pain, but
someone's got to do it

At the risk of sounding like my father, the best way to clean up is to not make too much mess in the first place. Be sure to put down heaps of newspaper—more than you think you'll need, because getting dried paint and stains out of clothes or carpets can be a monumental pain. Just because acrylic paints can be cleaned with water doesn't mean they won't leave some sort of mark, particularly the strong colors like reds and blues.

So before you start, consider the following:

- Put down heaps of newspaper. I know I've just said this but it bears repeating. Try as you might, you are going to make a mess.

- Have a couple of cloths handy. I personally cut up old towels, but if that's too 1947 for you just buy a packet of kitchen cloths. I use these to clean off brushes when changing colors. I wipe my hands and remove spills with them too.

- Keep a jar of water nearby just in case you need it to rinse a brush or clean something up quickly.

- Make sure you aren't getting too carried away and flicking paint on the wall or floor. Let the moment take you by all means, but remember that you want to get your security deposit back and/or keep any cohabiters happy.

- Wear an old T-shirt or the 'funky' one that your brother gave you for your birthday. Either way it won't matter if it gets ruined. As for smocks, don't even think about it unless you're under ten.

- Consider your bottom half as well. Paint tends to end up in all sorts of unexpected places so pull out your old tracksuit pants and leave your nice jeans on the bedroom floor.

CLEANING BRUSHES

To maintain your brushes in pristine condition all you need to do is wipe off the excess paint, wash them in warm, soapy water and finish with a cold rinse. Use your fingers to smooth the bristles out and lay them on a sheet of newspaper to dry. If you have let paint dry on a brush you can try to clean it with acetone, but do so in a well-ventilated area and try to use as little as possible. It's toxic stuff. Wear some rubber gloves just to be on the safe side. Better still, consider it a lesson learned and buy a new brush after vowing never to do anything like that to your brushes again.

CLEANING PALETTES

I'm a fine one to give you advice on cleaning palettes because I'm crap at doing it myself. But if you like your palette to look immaculate at every outing, all you need to do is wipe it down with a cloth then wash it in warm, soapy water. If the paint has dried you'll need some sort of pot scourer to scratch it off. Alternatively, you can be like me and just leave it to dry and simply keep squeezing new paint over old.

CLEANING SMOOTH SURFACES WITH DRIED PAINT ON THEM

This is an easy one. Just scratch the dried paint off with your fingernails or a table knife. Be careful not to hack away at the surface—it's not like you're back at your old school desk, calipers in hand.

CLEANING CLOTHES

I've never had to do this because my wardrobe is pretty cheap, so I asked a friend who works at a paint store and owns expensive clothes about this one. Here's what he recommended:

If the stain is fresh, hold the article of clothing under a tap of cold running water. Hold the bulk of the garment above the stain so the color doesn't spread. After you've managed to remove most of the paint, hold the garment over an old towel and soap up the stained area with ordinary household soap. Work the affected area by rubbing it between your thumb and forefinger, using a rolling action. Avoid rubbing the stain directly. Rinse the affected area under cold water and repeat the above procedure as many times as it takes to completely remove the stain. Once

CLEANING CARPETS

Now you shouldn't have this problem because I did tell you to put down heaps of newspaper. Acrylic paints are not that hard to remove as long as the paint hasn't completely dried. All you need to do is rinse the affected area immediately with water then sponge it out. Keep sponging and cleaning until the stain is removed. If the paint has dried, try to scratch it out with your fingernail or a kitchen knife. If that fails, you may have to use scissors to trim the carpet slightly, assuming the pile is deep enough. Don't get carried away and give your carpet a Number 1. I've done this and still managed to get my security deposit back. I also filled in the nail holes in the wall with toothpaste. Hey, you gotta do what you gotta do!

you're satisfied the stain is completely gone and you've calmed down a bit, wrap the garment in a towel and twist it to remove all the moisture. Hang up to dry.

With dried stains, soak the garment in lukewarm water for at least 15 minutes, using household soap or laundry detergent. Using the thumb and forefingers of both hands, work the affected area with the rolling action described on the previous page. As this releases the paint into the water, you will need to change the water a number of times. Do this as often as necessary, repeating the procedure. Some stubborn stains may need to be soaked overnight. Do not use hot water. Do not boil, dry clean or use solvents or thinners—these methods will only drive the stain in deeper. Do not iron over a stain. Don't machine wash, and keep stained garments separate from other washing.

Well said trusty paint-store man! I couldn't have put it better myself. And if I could have, I certainly wouldn't have used the words 'do not' quite so often.

CLEANING YOURSELF

Soap and water should do the trick, but if you have a stubborn stain or build-up of paint on your skin then mix a small amount of table sugar in with your soap. Wash as usual and you should find any stains or residue gone. Makes your skin nice and soft as well.

The top 10 mistakes weekend artists make ...

MISTAKE 1: I'll buy the three primary colors and then I'll mix all the colors I need!

REALITY: No you won't. Most novices know that blue and yellow makes green, but that's about as far as it goes. And do you think you'll really remember what proportions you mixed in case you run out of a color and need to make it again? Consider buying pre-mixed colors unless you really know how to mix the color you want.

MISTAKE 2: Even though the guy from the art store said not to buy primary colors I did anyway. He was right, I don't know how to mix them so I'll just make a yellow, red and blue painting!

REALITY: See, I told you! And now you're going to do some awful painting that looks like a bad high school project. Unless you're particularly skilled, anything you do with primary colors will eventually find itself out the front of your house on a distant household rubbish collection day.

MISTAKE 3: I've bought this pack of ten mixed paints so I'm ready to go!

REALITY: Just because you've bought a pack of ten paints doesn't mean you have to use them all at the same time on the one painting. If you're even the slightest bit uncertain about what colors to use just follow the Art Store Guy's 3-Color Rule (see page 24). But I'm also being a bit sneaky, because what I'm really trying to stop you doing is splashing a heap of random colors all over the place. After all, we want to do something that looks good on the wall in a relatively short amount of time.

MISTAKE 4: I'm just going have a go and see what happens!—PART 1

REALITY: I like the idea behind this one, but be prepared to have two goes. Painting is like anything—it's rare to hit your stride on the first attempt. So, if you do something that's a complete mess, clean up, pack up and have another go after a good snoozy/boozy night. No-one runs a marathon just by stepping out the front door. So by all means pack up—just don't give up.

MISTAKE 5: I'm just going have a go and see what happens!—PART 2

REALITY: Have a go but be sure to have some idea of what you're going to do. I didn't write this book for nothing you know! If you just go home and start slopping some paint around it's pretty certain that you'll give up and those paints will only see the light of day next time you're babysitting your nephews or nieces.

MISTAKE 6: This painting is looking good, but I'm going to keep going, and going, and going ...

REALITY: This is a dilemma. How do you know when the painting you're doing is finished? After you've been painting away for a bit, you will most likely reach a point where you like what you see. It can be tempting to just keep slapping paint on all over the place, but that's the time to stop, put down the brush and walk away. If you feel that you have to keep going then start doing another painting—that way you won't ruin the one you're already happy with. Remember, you can always go back to your original painting at a later date. It will still be there tomorrow, I promise.

MISTAKE 7: Top of the range everything will make me a better painter!

REALITY: While you do tend to get better coverage from more expensive paints, most people can spend a reasonable amount of money and still get good quality. And besides, not everyone has access to an art store. I suggest a range of moderate and cheaper products. There will be a bit of trial and error involved, but think of it as a learning experience. Even though I've tried lots of products I still buy duds every now and then. Don't feel you have to mortgage the cat to set yourself up.

MISTAKE 8: I'm not the creative type!

REALITY: Rubbish. I'm not the mathematical type, but I can still do a tax return because all I do is follow the instructions. And what do you think this book is full of? (Those of you with a smart answer to this question can keep it to yourselves.) Trust me, you're underestimating yourself.

MISTAKE 9: I don't need to put any newspaper down. I just want to get started!

REALITY: Now what was that about leading a horse to water?

MISTAKE 10: I like bright things. Do you think glitter is a good idea?

REALITY: No.

And onto the projects ...

So now you've got an idea of what acrylic painting is all about, we're moving onto the first lot of projects. I've listed what you need and provided step-by-step instructions to help you along. But don't feel that you have to do things to the letter. Maybe you'll want to change the color or modify the technique. Or maybe you'll even skip a step here and there, and still be happy with the result. That's fine with me. These projects can be used as either instructions or general guidelines. Just go with how you're feeling at the time.

So, if your final painting looks just like the one in the picture, then congratulations! And if it looks nothing like the one in the picture, then you have my congratulations as well!

ROOT VEGETABLES AND THEIR ROLE IN ART

I've never read an art book that gives any credence to the humble potato—it's about time someone did. Think about it. Almost everyone has at some stage picked up a sliced potato, dipped it in some brightly colored paint and stamped away on a piece of paper. The teacher would then peg it up until it dried and get you to sign your name. You would then rush home proudly to mom and she would stick it on the refrigerator for all to see.

A painting and an exhibition all in 24 hours. Aahh, those were good times.

For some the potato is the beginning and the end of their artistic endeavors, which is why I thought it was only appropriate that I start my projects where many of you will have left off—printing with a potato. Although I'm starting with a potato, I'm also going to show you how to create other printed designs and patterns using other things from your kitchen. The application may change but the technique remains the same. The other thing that remains the same, no matter how old you are, is that niggling sense of pride you feel when you've actually made something yourself. Kids don't tend to wonder if they're doing the right thing—they just get stuck in. So think like a child for a couple of hours, but please don't pick your nose and be sure to wash your hands after going to the toilet. And I mean properly.

These **PROJECTS** can be used as either instructions or general guidelines.

PROJECT 1

POTATO PRINT BLOSSOMS

You say potato, I say Japanese cherry blossom tree. I went through the entire contents of my crisper in order to get this design. I tried peppers, carrots and even some just-about-to-turn-mouldy broccoli before returning to the perennial kindergarten favorite. I rather enjoyed seeing the various effects you get with different vegetables, and that's half the fun of painting—experimenting and seeing what happens. For some of you, this project may also be your first foray into painting. If you're a bit uncertain at this point just follow my instructions to the letter. If you don't like the colors I've used, then try it in colors that you do like. Don't look for excuses not to put brush to canvas. I don't want to get all Oprah on you, but the point of this is to just have a go! You've got to start somewhere, so why not here? Don't think about it too much and don't worry about mistakes. If it doesn't work, just paint over it and start again tomorrow. Think of this as the project that's going to get you out of the starting gate. Giddy-up!

Get this:

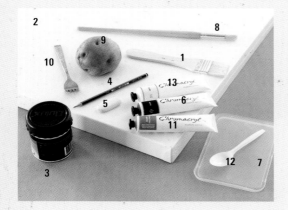

1. Medium sized flat brush

2. 24" x 30" pre-stretched canvas

3. 8 fl oz tester pot of pale gray acrylic paint

4. HB pencil

5. Eraser

6. Tube of black acrylic paint

7. Takeout container lid

8. Round hog hair brush, size 9

9. Medium sized potato (try and get a roundish looking one)

10. Fork

11. Tube of magenta acrylic paint

12. Plastic spoon

13. Tube of white acrylic paint

Step 1

Put down plenty of newspaper. Using the flat brush, paint the canvas with two coats of pale gray acrylic paint. Allow it to dry between coats. Lightly sketch the tree's outline with the pencil, eraser at hand—use the main picture on page 55 as a guide. Squeeze some black acrylic paint onto the container lid. Dip the hog hair brush in and paint the outline of the tree's trunk and branches. Add the smaller branches and twigs. Allow to dry. Erase any stray lines. Wash the container lid.

Step 3

Begin stamping the canvas with the potato. Don't get too carried away with the number of blossoms. We're aiming for eastern subtlety not German measles. Allow to dry.

Step 2

Cut the potato in half. Stick the fork securely into the potato so you can easily dip and print. Don't force it all the way through the flesh as we don't want the fork jabbing the canvas. Squeeze a big dollop of magenta acrylic paint on to the container lid and spread it out with the plastic spoon. Dip the potato into the paint.

TIPS

■ It's important to cut the potato evenly in half so there is a nice flat area that will allow the paint to be distributed consistently.

■ Okay, if you haven't cut the potato evenly then you may find that not enough paint is being left behind and the effect is very patchy as opposed to pretty. Try the following technique: when you stamp the potato twist it slightly to increase the amount of paint left on the canvas. You can also cheat a little by dipping your finger in the paint and dabbing those blossoms that need a bit of touching up.

■ Throw the potato out after you've finished. Paint doesn't taste quite as good as butter, or so I'm told.

Step 4

Repeat Step 3 using white paint. Overlap a few blossoms to create another dimension. Allow to dry.

PROJECT 2

CUPPA ART

One of the common misconceptions about art is that you need all sorts of fancy equipment. Don't you need an easel and a set of sable brushes? And of course you'll need a complete range of colors, right? Wrong! Objects that can be used for painting are often right in front of you, particularly if you like a cup of tea in the morning. The point of this project is also to show you that not every painting has to be a massive show stopper. These small canvases are really quick to do and look rather cute when there's a number of them. You don't even have to hang them, just put them on a mantelpiece or shelf and they're good to go. And all you need are three colors to get the job done. You'll probably find that once you start you'll get your own ideas about how to do this project. As my parents never said to me (although I wish they had) you're more creative than you think you are.

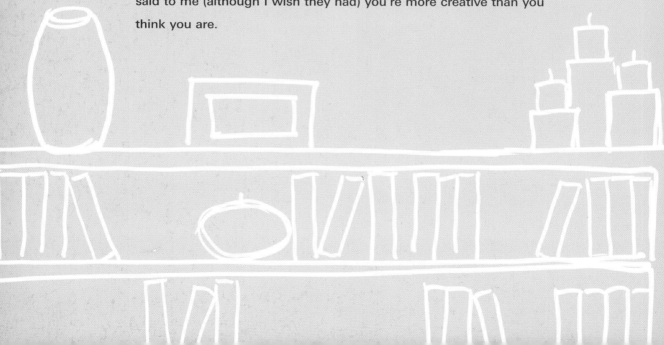

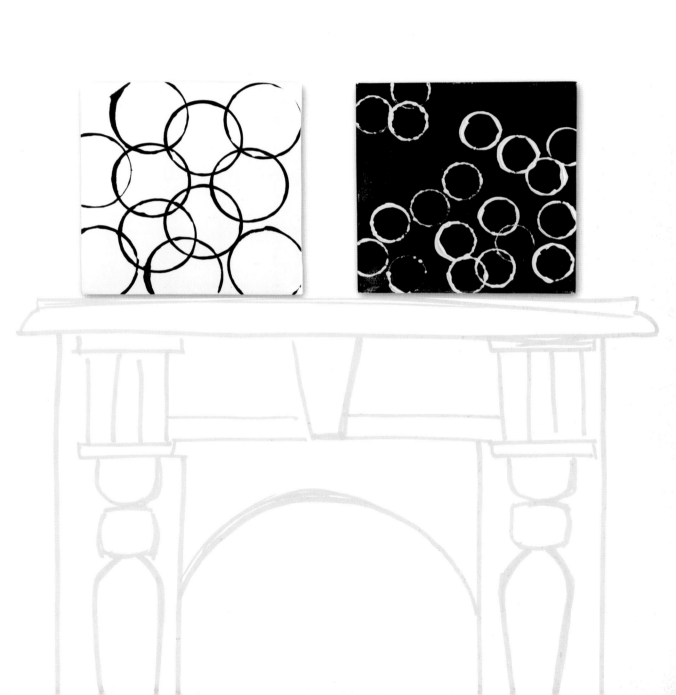

Get this:

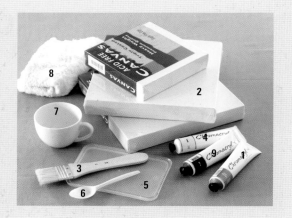

Step 1

Put down plenty of newspaper. Blob the grey acrylic paint directly on to the 7" x 7" canvas and brush it out with the flat brush. Don't forget to do the sides as well. Allow to dry. And add another coat so there's a nice opaque color.

1. Tube of neutral grey acrylic paint

2. Small pre-stretched canvases. (I used 7" x 7" & 10" x 10".)

3. Medium sized flat brush

4. Tube of white acrylic paint

5. Takeout container lid

6. Plastic spoon

7. Teacup

8. Cloth

9. Tube of black acrylic paint

Step 3

Now for the white 10" x 10" square canvas. Blob the white acrylic paint directly on the canvas and brush it out as in Step 1. Okay, I don't mind if you don't do a second coat.

Step 2

Squeeze some white acrylic paint on to the container lid and smooth it out with the plastic spoon. Now dip the cup in and stamp onto the canvas. Repeat a few times. You may get a build up of paint on the cup while you're stamping so just give it a quick wipe with the cloth and just keep on stamping. Set aside to dry and wash the takeout container lid and cup while you're waiting.

Variation Although I've used only two colors per canvas why not try adding a third?

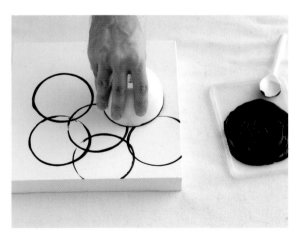

Step 4

Using a clean container lid, squirt out the black paint and spread it around with the plastic spoon. Dip the cup in and get stampin' just like you did before. Allow to dry and place both canvases on the shelf. Stand back. Admire.

TIPS

- Remember that a cup has two ends so try with both. You can get a smaller, thicker circle with the base of the cup — see the main picture (right) on page 59 for an example.

- Exercise some restraint with the number of stamps you do. Remember, you don't have to cover the whole canvas and in this case it'll probably look a whole lot better if you don't.

PROJECT 3

HIT THE BOTTLE

The idea for this project came to me when I was doing the experiments for the Potato Print Blossoms on pages 56–57. I was in my kitchen seeing if I could get a decent print from a sliced pepper (you can't). I had a lot of paint left over so I grabbed an olive oil bottle to see what would happen. Before I knew it another project was born. This artwork is a favorite because it was one of the projects I first submitted to the publisher in my proposal for this book, so I'm glad that pepper turned out to be a dud stamp after all. It can be frustrating when things don't go to plan, but frequently that forces you to find another, better way. I often get customers in the store wanting to know what will be the outcome if they mix this with that, or try this with that. The answer is that there is no answer—you just have to give it a shot and see what happens. The thing about experimentation is that you never know what is going to happen, and that's the great and annoying thing about it.

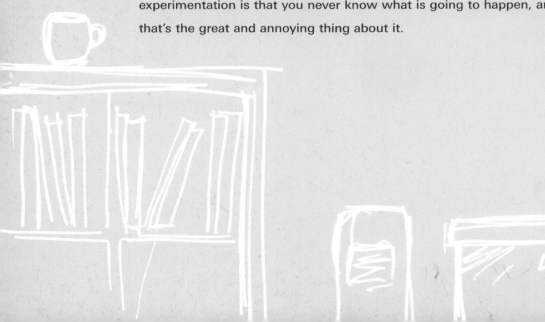

Get this:

1. Medium sized flat brush

2. 24" x 36" pre-stretched canvas

3. 2 x 8 fl oz pots of ultramarine blue acrylic paint

4. Tube of cadmium red hue acrylic paint

5. Takeout container lid

6. Plastic spoon

7. Olive oil bottle, but anything with a square base will do.

8. Cloth

9. Water-based gloss varnish

10. Plastic cup

Step 1

Put down plenty of newspaper. Using the flat brush, paint the the canvas with a coat of the ultramarine blue acrylic paint. The color may look patchy at first but don't panic, this diminishes after you apply three (yes three) coats. Allow it to dry between coats. Clean the brush. Put a blob of the red acrylic paint on the container lid and spread it around with the plastic spoon so you have an even blob of paint.

Step 4

Continue making rows but don't completely cover the canvas. Just leave a section unpatterned, as it adds an interesting contrast to the patterned area. Allow to dry.

Step 2

Dip the bottom of the olive oil bottle into the paint.

Step 3

Stamp a row of squares along the side of the canvas. Repeat this dip-and-stamp process on subsequent rows. Don't worry if the rows aren't straight — it will add interest to the final design. You may find paint builds up on the base of the bottle. If this happens, use the cloth to give it a quick wipe and resume your stamping frenzy.

Step 5

Pour some water-based gloss varnish into the plastic cup. Using the flat brush paint two coats of varnish over the whole canvas. It goes on milky at first but dries clear with a high-sheen finish. Allow to dry between coats.

TIPS

■ I know that three coats of paint sounds a lot but you have to trust me. Ultramarine blue is a semi-opaque paint and it builds up to a strong translucent and patchy blue that gives another dimension to the background.

■ You don't have to use an olive oil bottle. There are plenty of other bottles out there that can make an interesting shape. Go to your kitchen cupboard and see what else you could use.

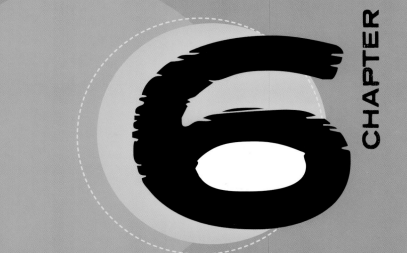

Inspiration

One of the biggest problems for new artists is deciding what to paint. Often people will come into the store, clutching a magazine picture, and tell me that they want to "paint this." All plagiarism issues aside, they're on the right track because clearly they've seen something that has inspired them to the point of having a go. Although it's said that imitation is the sincerest form of flattery, not too many artists are flattered by the thought of someone else ripping off their work. Still, we all have to start somewhere. Anyway, it's pretty rare that a beginner can copy the work of a more experienced artist. What usually happens is they start to copy, quickly realize they can't quite get it right, and then start doing their own thing. And that's the way it should be.

So, if you'd like to paint something but don't know what, the most obvious thing to do is look at other paintings. Visit a few galleries or look at a few art books. Or get online and have a look. Remember, you're not looking for things to copy, you're looking for things that catch your eye. It could be the color, it could be the shape, it could be the size—as long as it appeals to you. Make a point of collecting five things that you like the look of. You'll probably find that there is something familiar about the things you like. See, already you're showing evidence that you have your own eye. With all the prepackaged taste magazines we have today it's often hard for people to define what they actually like, as opposed to what they think they should like, or what is currently fashionable. I'm trying to encourage you to develop your own eye, but do feel free to borrow someone else's until we get yours up and running.

Inspiration also conjures up all sorts of mythological notions of muses descending from the heavens to kiss ideas into unsuspecting artists. For those of you who don't know your Greek mythology, the muses are the nine daughters of Zeus who descend from Helicon to inspire artists, poets and musicians. Anyway, that's where the expression 'kissed by a muse' originates. As much as I love the

role magical mythology plays in explaining inspiration, the reality is often considerably more prosaic. For example, I was eating a packet of potato chips the other day and as I was binning the empty packet I spotted a discarded plastic sheet with some cats drawn on it. So I did a discreet double take, quickly picked up the sheet and shoved it in my bag. It's now in my scrapbook that I flick through when looking for ideas. I use this example, because it shows that inspiration can strike anywhere, anytime. Even I didn't expect one of the daughters of Zeus to be hanging around an overflowing public bin, waiting to kiss my chip-crumbed mouth. Maybe she'd had a rough night.

SOURCES OF INSPIRATION

Art galleries—an obvious choice that comes top of the list.

Art books—these are good sources for ideas but the prices can be astronomical. Still, if you love the artist it's worth the expense. The good thing about many bookstores these days is that they actually encourage you to sit and read. So take advantage of that and perhaps jot down a few color combinations you like, or sketch a couple of ideas, when no one's looking.

Real-estate magazines—I look through these regularly, and not only to remind myself that I'll be renting for the rest of my life. I also look at any wall paintings that may be hanging in the advertised properties. (But what I really want to know is why people with enormous panoramic views fill their houses with furniture from IKEA stores? What is that all about?)

Advertising catalogs—furniture catalogs are good because they often have printed materials and soft furnishings in them. Look for patterns and colors that you like. Just because it's not on a canvas doesn't mean you can't put it on one yourself!

Interior-design magazines—these are expensive but worth it. You will always find something you are inspired by when looking on the walls of the featured houses.

Libraries—it's old school to go to a library rather than jump on a computer, but remember that not everything is online. Interior decoration books from the 1960s and 1970s always interest me. If you can get past the ridiculously dated rooms, look on the walls and check out the art—some of the designs and color combinations can be so old that they appear new and fresh. Many libraries also carry a range of interior-design magazines to borrow if you don't want to go out and buy them.

Second-hand bookstores—if there's one thing I love about living in Sydney, it's hanging around disheveled old bookstores on rainy days. Have a look for old art and interior-design books. Sometimes, if you're lucky, you might find a personal message in the front of the book. You know what I mean, "with love, from Scotty," or some such thing. It's like a little peek into the book's past and always makes me wonder where the book has been and how it's ended up on these shelves.

Office doodles!—those meetings may be boring you to death but the doodles you did at the top of the handout should be kept for later reference. After a while, you'll start to see just what a distinctive style you have and just how many dire meetings you've endured.

KEEPING A VISUAL DIARY
(Even If It's Not Actually A Visual Diary)

One way to generate ideas is to keep a visual diary of some sort. It's a great way of putting all your ideas and inspirations in one place. With all the choices we have today, a diary doesn't have be a fancy leather-bound book. It can simply be a plain old exercise book, for all I care. What you need to do is find some way of recording things that catch your eye. I actually use children's scrapbooks for this. They're big, cheap and lightweight. When I'm not digging things out of bins (I only did that once, okay?) I rip things out of magazines and glue them down in random order. I also put my own notes and ideas next to them. While writing *Artful Spaces*, I kept a small notepad next to my bed and when I would wake up I'd scribble down any ideas I'd had during the night. Seemingly that's when my brain does all its creative ruminations.

OTHER VERSIONS OF A VISUAL DIARY

If an actual visual diary doesn't sound like you, then how about trying one of the following:

- Use a good old manila folder to shove things into. You don't have to cut or glue anything.

- A desktop folder on your computer: spend a lunch hour surfing the net and drop a few images into a desktop folder.

- I recently bought a mobile phone with a camera and it's the best thing since sliced bread. If I see something I like, be it a piece of graffiti or a pattern of some sort, I just whip out the phone and snap away. Of course, you shouldn't do this in art galleries, but anywhere else is fair game as far as I'm concerned. I've snapped art in office foyers, store windows and even pages out of library books. I know I'd have more integrity if I stopped and did a brief sketch, but right now my mobile-phone camera works for me.

VISUAL DIARY TIPS
(Whatever Format You Use)

1. Don't feel you have to use just one method to record your ideas. You can sketch concepts, glue in pictures, add color with pencils or markers. You can even use good old ballpoint pens if you want to. Just use whatever's handy.

2. It doesn't have to look all nice and clean and properly cut. In fact, the more messy, torn and random it is the better it looks. This can be hard to get over if you pride yourself on being orderly and systematic in the office, but you'll get used to it. I went through this and can still remember the days when I felt like I was being a counter-culture radical as I tore things out of magazines rather than neatly cutting them with scissors. Sad but true.

3. Try to record the idea as soon as you see/get it. This is one reason why camera phones are just so brilliant. You see it, you snap it, and there it is. Not all ideas are based directly on something you've seen. In those instances I've been known to write or draw things on the back of scrap paper. Otherwise, I know I'll completely forget. I just glue my musings into my scrapbook that night where they wait for my future reference.

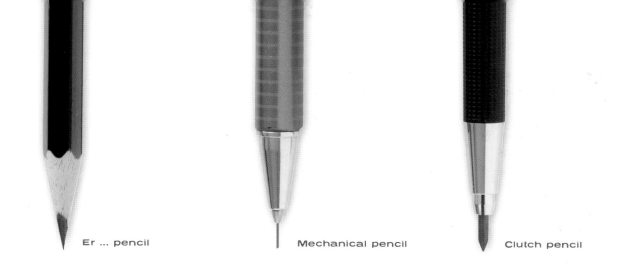

Er ... pencil

Mechanical pencil

Clutch pencil

SKETCHY TYPES WITH SHADY INTENTIONS

Although it's not my cup of gin, I know there are people out there who will want to keep a traditional visual diary and do lots of little sketches. Here's a few things to help you folks out.

2B OR NOT 2B. (Now Where Have I Heard That Before?)

Most people are familiar with HB pencils because that's what they used at school, but art stores carry a complete range of pencils which can be a tad confusing if the only one you've used is the regulation HB school pencil.

Pencils are divided into two categories. They are B and H.

The B series are softer and leave a darker line, while the H gang are a tougher bunch and are good for finer lines in lighter shades of gray. As you can see, a HB is right in the middle and so is a good all-rounder. You will notice that I always recommend them for drawing lines and guides on canvas because they don't leave a lot of color (like a B pencil will) or potentially dent the canvas surface (like a H pencil can).

But back to sketching. If you want to sketch then start with a 2B and 4B and see how things go. The only problem with pencils is that you always have to keep sharpening them, so buy a pencil sharpener while you're at it. And make sure you get one with a little container attached to it so you're not leaving shavings all over the place—all because you couldn't be bothered walking to the bin.

Extremely hard
9H to 7H

Very hard
6H to 5H

Hard
4H to 3H

Medium hard
2H to H

Medium
F to HB

Medium soft
B to 2B

Soft
3B to 4B

Very soft
5B to 6B

Extremely soft
7B to 9B

MECHANICAL PENCILS

These are those clicky-clicky pencils that look something like a pen. These are often called propeling pencils and come in standard lead widths of approximately 0.3, 0.5, 0.7 and 0.9—the higher the number the larger the lead width. The accompanying leads also come in the B and H versions, just like regular pencils, although the range is limited because of the finer lead size. A plus is that these pencils require no sharpening.

I've never really liked propeling pencils because I press down firmly when I draw and the leads always break. I was whining to the manager the other day about it and he suggested I use a 0.7 or 0.9 instead of the usual 0.5. And you know, he was right. All those years I've wasted …

CLUTCH PENCILS

Clutch pencils are similar to propeling pencils only with a larger 2 mm width lead. They do need to be sharpened, so if you decide to buy one make sure it has a sharpener built into the end so you don't have to buy a specialist sharpener to do the job. The refill leads come in a range of grades and can be a bit expensive if you go through them like crazy. Still, they are an option for those of you who like a sturdy technical pencil with thicker leads.

SKETCHPADS

If you decide that you'd like to carry a sketchpad consider the size and the weight of the one you buy. Those nicely bound ones with solid covers do look good but can feel too heavy if you have to lug them around all day. Spiral bound pads are much lighter even if they don't look as classy (I hate that word— whenever something is described as classy it inevitably looks like crud). As far as size goes I think a 6" x 8" pad is a good start; it's small enough for you to discreetly whip out almost anywhere and sketch away. Try not to go any smaller or else you'll feel like you're doing a picture book for a mouse.

PAPER SIZES

Although I'm not going to go into it in any great depth, I thought I'd provide you with a quick rundown of North American paper sizes.

	inches	mm
Letter	8½ x 11	216 x 279
Legal	8½ x 14	216 x 356
Ledger	17 x 11	432 x 279
Tabloid	11 x 17	279 x 432

There is an additional paper size called "government-letter"– 8½" x 10½" (76mm x 267mm). This paper size is used for children's writing and is commonly found in spiral-bound notebooks.

I hope you don't mind me asking, but what do you find inspiring?

I thought I'd take a random survey of a few friends and customers to see how other people get their ideas.

"Have an idea of what you want to do, but allow the possibilities of the medium to come into the concept itself."

Felix, Painter

"I think the world is in a sorry state at the moment. I'm using red, black and white paints. Black for the dark side of life, white for hope and red to represent bloodshed."

Eric, Painter

"Work from life. Sometimes I look through magazines for a color or a shape I can use. Mostly I paint from feelings—I've got to be happy with what I'm doing."

Terry, Painter

"My inspiration comes from within. I don't really look at the outside world. My paintings sort of develop themselves. It's about how I feel so it's truly abstract and non-representational."

Chris, Painter

"A bottle of Jack Daniels after dinner."

Tesha, Printmaker

"Cats and how they move and relate to their environment. The feline form really interests me."

Mary-Ann, Ceramicist

"Discussing an idea with other artists."

Evan, Painter

"Anything can inspire me. I usually get fixated on a few seemingly unrelated things. Like toffee apples, ivy and brick walls. At the moment it's all about mushrooms, old seventies electric organs and tree stumps—I like creating strange environments made up of these disparate objects."

Kylie, Painter

"I find inspiration in what surrounds me and the moments you spend just doing everyday activities. I recently did a painting based on the stains on the wall surrounding one of my light switches."

Stephanie, Painter

"I don't have time for this. I'm doubled parked!"

The unknown (and slightly irate) customer

Masked, man

I often get requests from new weekend artists wanting to paint something with stripes. If you are one of these people then using masking tape is an absolute must. Masking tape is a cream colored white tape that is basically a roll of paper with an adhesive side. All you do is put it on the canvas, paint away, then rip the tape off and you'll be left with a sharp, straight edge (although, if truth be known, you will most likely have to do a minor touch up here and there as some of that darned paint always seems to migrate under the tape—until you get the technique down pat).

Now, I also have a confession to make about painted stripes on canvas: I think they suck, and not in a good way. Stripes always look like beach towels on the wall to me. However, I do like geometric shapes. I've never met a square, a triangle or an oblong that I didn't like and the good news is they can all be created using the masking technique. So if a customer gives me the old "I'd like to paint stripes" line I always try and steer them in the direction of other geometric patterns. After I sketch a few quick examples, those stripe dreams are a distant memory and the world is a better place for it.

I think one of the reasons people like stripes is because no one has shown them what else they can do, which is a shame because masking can create endless possibilities. Geometric shapes can just be patterns or they can actually look like something as well. When we get to the projects you'll see what I mean.

Masking is also a perfect way to demonstrate the Art Store Guy's 3-Color Rule. Although I don't use it in every project I'll let you know when I do.

While there are specialist art masking tapes these are not easy to get hold of, although I have seen them at painting trade centers. Ordinary masking tape is easy to find, so I'm going to show you how to work with that. It's also cheap and comes in a variety of widths. In order to get the best result you can't just stick, paint and rip. There is a technique involved—have a look at the opposite page to see how it's done.

Masking can create **ENDLESS POSSIBILITIES**. Geometric shapes can just be patterns or they can actually look like something as well.

STICK, PAINT AND RIP—THE RIGHT WAY TO DO IT

Step 1

First, pull out the length of tape you need. Place it on the canvas, making sure it stays in a straight line. Now run your finger FIRMLY—and I mean FIRMLY—along the edge of the tape to ensure it is stuck down enough to minimize paint creeping in under the edge.

Step 2

When you paint along the tape be sure to push the brush away from the masking tape; we don't want too much paint to seep under the tape and wreck our straight line.

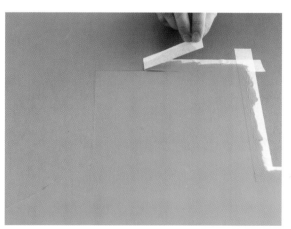

Step 3

When the paint is dry, remove the tape slowly. You're not waxing your legs (or whatever) here. The aim is to take it slow and remove the tape in one piece. It will just save you trying to scrape away small pieces of tape that can remain if you get too gung ho when ripping the tape off.

Step 4

Use a small brush to do any touch ups. It's almost inevitable that you'll have to do this, when you first start out.

IMPORTANT TIP: If you place masking tape over an existing painted surface you must ensure that the paint underneath is completely dry. If it isn't, you will most likely find that when you rip the tape off half the paint will come away with it. And that's gonna piss you right off.

Masking is easy now that I've told you how to do it. Still, you might want to have a couple of test runs on the side of your pre-stretched canvas before you get stuck into the front. The main thing is to get the tape stuck down firmly enough to minimize the amount of touching up you'll have to do. It does take practice until you get the whole pressure/stickiness thing worked out, but it's not rocket science— you can easily master the process after a couple of attempts.

There are also two basic ways to use masking tape:

1 To create specific geometric shapes. Paint a triangle, square or oblong by using one side of the masking tape as a masking border.

2 To create a line the thickness of the tape. By this I mean putting down the tape and painting over both sides of it. You then remove it and have a stripe (shudder) the width of the tape.

I'll be having a go with both in the projects. And speaking of projects here come some now …

MAYBE NEXT WEEKEND ...

I assume because you're reading this book that you have some interest in creating something artistic. Now stop treating this bookstore as a library and take this book to the sales desk! Just kidding. But seriously, some people will get all fired up and go home and get stuck in, while others will never quite get around to it because they're waiting for the right mood to strike them.

I personally think the concept of being in the right mood is highly overrated. Look at it this way, most people do not bound out of bed in the morning because they're in the mood to go to work. No, they have a shower, quickly down a coffee and show up at their desk. And before they know it they've had a productive, even enjoyable day with a few small victories and laughs along the way. What I'm trying to say is that if you just start doing something you'll get into the swing of it. A few coats of paint on that canvas and I can virtually guarantee you'll be hooked. Just be businesslike about it and schedule some time to get started on one of these projects. Don't wait for some mythical mood to strike you. Sometimes the less you think the better you'll do.

PROJECT 1

BASIC GEOMETRIC YELLOW AND WHITE

Although I have mentioned the value of a number of paintings to fill a wall, the fact remains that some of you will want one big painting. Well, here it is. There isn't a whole lot of paint involved, and this could easily be done in a day. A minimalist painting that takes minimal work and a minimal amount of paint. Can't argue with that. A lot of people will wonder what this painting actually is, but the fact is that it's not anything at all—it's just some yellow shapes on a white background. To be honest, I just wanted to use the color yellow! That's the thing about art, it's open to interpretation, and just because I don't see anything in this doesn't mean there isn't something in it for other people. So if someone asks you "What's it supposed to be?" Just reply "What do you think?" Their answer might show you something that you didn't even know was there.

Get this:

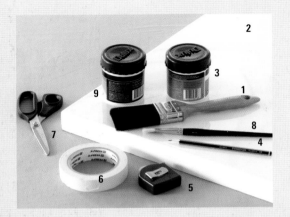

1. Medium sized house painting brush

2. 36" x 48" pre-stretched canvas

3. 8 fl oz tester pot of white acrylic paint

4. HB pencil

5. Tape measure

6. Masking tape

7. Scissors

8. ¾" flat synthetic brush

9. 8 fl oz tester pot of yellow acrylic paint

Step 1

Put down plenty of newspaper. Using the house painting brush, paint the canvas with two coats of white acrylic paint. Allow it to dry between coats. Use the HB pencil and tape measure to draw small marks that roughly correspond with the finished image on page 81 — or for more accurate measurements see page 222. (Or go crazy and come up with your own design.)

Step 3

Using the ¾" flat synthetic brush apply 2–3 coats of yellow acrylic paint to the masked section (including the sides) and allow to dry between coats.

Step 2

Place the masking tape firmly along the pencil marks. Take it down the sides of the canvas. You can use your fingers to tear off the masking tape or grab the pair of scissors to do the job.

Variation The variation for this artwork is to simply turn it on its side. Yep, something as mundane as that can make all the difference to how you see your art. Although I show the projects from one perspective in the photos, feel free to turn your version upside down or sideways. I guess it all comes back to that open-to-individual-interpretation thing. Just because I like it one way doesn't mean that you should. It's not about what's right, it's about what's right for you.

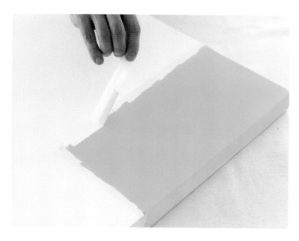

Step 4

Gently remove the tape and touch up any yellow paint blobs that may have snuck under the tape and cover any obvious pencil marks with paint.

PROJECT 2

3-COLOR SQUARE GEOMETRIC

Triptych. I didn't really know what it meant either until I started working in an art store, but it simply means an image made up of three sections. And while we're talking of things made up of threes, I may as well go the whole hog and make this project in colors using the 3-color rule. Does this mean the best things in life are three? Or just that I crack crap jokes at any opportunity? I have been recommending projects like this to customers for ages, but this is the first time I've actually had to do it for myself. As usual, it's easy to tell someone what to do in theory, but until you do it yourself you don't realize what could be done to make it better and easier. My humble apologies to any of you who took my advice in the store and found that things didn't quite go as planned …

Get this:

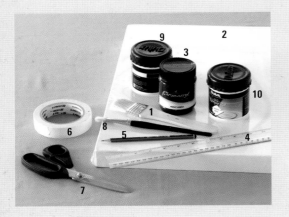

1. Medium sized flat brush

2. Three 20" x 20" pre-stretched canvases

3. 8 fl oz pot of burnt umber paint

4. Ruler

5. HB pencil

6. Roll of masking tape

7. Scissors

8. ¾" flat synthetic brush

9. 8 fl oz tester pot of medium blue paint

10. 8 fl oz tester pot of light blue acrylic paint

Step 1

Put down plenty of newspaper. Using the medium sized flat brush, paint one of the canvases with two coats of burnt umber acrylic paint. Allow it to dry. Now get out your ruler and HB pencil then lightly draw a couple of small marks 8" in from the right side of the canvas. Place the masking tape firmly along this line, taking the tape right down the sides. Cut the masking tape using the scissors.

Step 4

Draw a second line 8" from the bottom of the canvas. Tape this line again as per Step 1, and paint this section with two coats of light blue paint, allowing time to dry between coats.

Step 2

Using the ¾" flat synthetic brush, paint inside the tape with medium blue paint. You may need to do two coats, depending on the coverage of your paint. Allow it to dry between coats.

Step 3

Ensure the painted section is completely dry before removing the tape and touching up any stray blobs of paint or obvious pencil marks.

Step 5

When all is dry remove the tape, doing the touch up thing if necessary. Now repeat these steps on the remaining two canvases using the same three colors but painted in a different sequence for each canvas.

Variation There are endless possibilities with this project. Remember the color examples in the Art Store Guy's 3-Color Rule? Here's some of them again to jog your memory.

PROJECT 3

CITY PROFILE

I have a confession to make. I think man-made objects are more interesting than those made by mother nature. There, I've said it. Don't get me wrong, I'm all for preserving our natural environment, and I do draw some of my ideas from natural landscapes, but it's just that I've never seen a tree that was more impressive than a skyscraper or a field that was more interesting to me than a city street. That's not to say I don't like to visit the country—I most certainly do, and I spend quite a bit of time there. I'm always happy to visit the country but I'm just as happy to get back to the city. Even though some people find skyscrapers ugly, I always think they look rather smart. It's almost as if mother nature has dressed up and put on a suit and decided to carry a briefcase. But it's good to know the plants, trees and soil are still under there somewhere.

Get this:

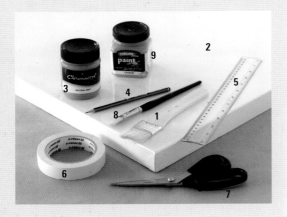

1. Medium sized flat brush

2. 24" x 36" pre-stretched canvas

3. 8 fl oz pot of neutral grey acrylic paint

4. HB pencil

5. Ruler

6. Masking tape

7. Scissors

8. ¾" flat synthetic brush

9. 8 fl oz pot of orange acrylic paint

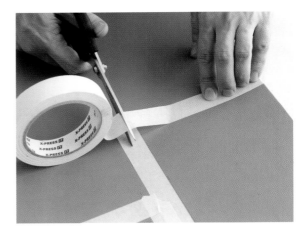

Step 1

Put down plenty of newspaper. Using the flat brush, paint the canvas with two coats of neutral gray acrylic paint. Allow it to dry between coats. Using the HB pencil and ruler, draw lines to roughly correspond to the image on page 89—or for more accurate measurements see page 222. Use the scissors to cut off the masking tape.

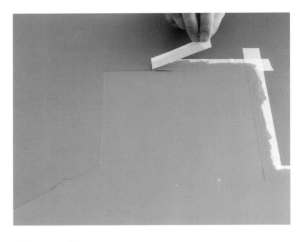

Step 3

Slowly remove the masking tape.

Step 2

Using the ¾" flat synthetic brush, apply as many coats of orange acrylic paint as needed to ensure you have a solid orange color. I found long vertical strokes work best — said the vicar to the milkmaid! But seriously folks, because I used a cheap student quality paint I had to do four coats to achieve the opaque finish I wanted, but it was worth it in the end. Allow time to dry between coats.

Step 4

Touch up any orange paint blobs that may have snuck under the tape. Also paint over any obvious pencil lines with the gray acrylic paint. I tried to remove them with an eraser but found that it tended to rub away some of the paint color. You may also be lazy like me and leave the pencil marks there as you'll find they blend into the gray background anyway.

PROJECT 4

TWO TAPES AND
TWO COLORS

I was trying to think up another project idea for this chapter but nothing was springing to mind, so I decided to move onto other things and left it for a couple of weeks. Then I arrived home one day to find the back door of my house smashed to bits. Yep, I'd been broken into. So as I sat there waiting for the cops to arrive I began to sketch on an old newspaper on the table and before I knew it another idea was born. The glass in the door had broken into a series of small triangles, and I eventually used that idea in this project. I'm sure few people feel like sketching after having been robbed, but I must say I was considerably relieved to find that the computer was still there, the DVD player remained in its place, and the digital camera was still where I'd left it. The only things stolen were the coins in my change bowl and … a pair of tracksuit pants. Well, at least the cops had a good laugh.

Get this:

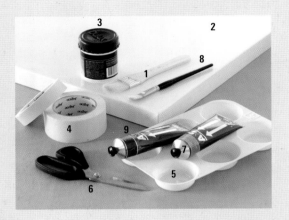

1. Medium sized flat brush

2. 24" x 30" pre-stretched canvas

3. 8 fl oz tester pot of beige paint

4. 2 rolls of masking tape with different widths.
   I used 1" & 2".

5. Deep well kids palette

6. Scissors

7. Tube of cadmium red hue acrylic paint

8. ¾" flat synthetic brush

9. Tube of ivory black acrylic paint

Step 1

Put down plenty of newspaper. Using the flat brush, paint the canvas with two coats of beige acrylic paint. Allow it to dry between coats. Put one strip of the larger masking tape across the canvas about two-thirds of the way down.

Step 4

Repeat Step 3 with the ivory black acrylic paint on the remaining third of the canvas.

Step 2

Place some strips of the larger masking tape at angles in the top section of the painting. Press all these pieces down firmly, particularly along the outer edges. Repeat the process with the thinner tape on the remaining third of the canvas. You can use your fingers to tear off the masking tape or grab a pair of scissors to do the job. I'm a scissors man myself.

Step 3

Squeeze some red hue acrylic paint into the palette. Using the ¾" synthetic brush, paint the top section. Don't just slop it all over the place, you'll still have to use the technique I outlined at the beginning of this chapter (page 77). Allow to dry and do a repeat coat so it doesn't look crazily patchy. Wash the brush out and allow both the brush and the painted canvas to dry.

Step 5

When the whole thing is dry remove the tape (slowly now!) and do any small touch-ups if paint has seeped under the tape.

INSPIRATION

Although I could have used the 3-color rule here I didn't, which may make you wonder where I get alternative color ideas from. The colors for this project came from Soviet propaganda posters that I happened to stumble upon while online. I thought the graphic nature of this project and the strong colors of such posters made perfect partners—or should I say comrades?

Mediums
well done

One of the great myths about acrylic paints is that they are not as versatile as oil paints. Phooey, I say! Once upon a time this was certainly true, but things have changed. This is where mediums come into the picture. A medium is a product that you add to acrylic paint to change and enhance the qualities of the paint. With the right medium you can make the paint thicker, thinner, more translucent, or even increase the drying time. There are so many mediums available, but for reasons of economy I'm only going to deal with my personal favorite. It's called gel medium.

When I mention mediums to customers for the first time they always look a little worried. Mediums can be intimidating at first. For a start, there's a lot of them and sometimes that can be overwhelming in itself. And then there's the problem with what you actually do with them. I understand all this completely. The first time I bought a gel medium it sat on my shelf for about six months before I had the courage to open it up only to find that it had dried rock hard. I was so annoyed that I bought a new pot the next day and started to experiment only to discover all the great things I had been missing.

GEL MEDIUM

One of the common complaints about acrylic paints is that they lack the transparency and depth of oil colors. People often moan that the colors look much better wet and far too flat when they dry. Obviously these whiners haven't heard of gel medium, which is the answer to these problems.

Gel medium is a thick white substance that you add to acrylic colors to give them transparency and texture. Basically, it makes the paint thicker and clearer. The great thing about gel medium is that you can scrape and scratch away at it to produce some interesting textural effects that dry to a clear glossy wet-look finish.

COMMON QUESTIONS ABOUT GEL MEDIUM

How do I use it?

Put a big blob in a plastic cup and add a touch of acrylic paint. Don't go too heavy with the paint, because the more paint you add the lesser the transparency effect. Mix the two together until they form an even pastel version of the paint. As a general guide I'd say add one part paint to ten parts gel medium, although you can change those ratios depending upon the effect you're after.

Are you sure it dries clear? It's white in the tub.

Yes it does. I don't know how this happens but I guess some magic robot sorts that out at the factory.

Can I use it on its own for a thick, clear, resin-like effect?

Unfortunately no. I tried this out myself. If you put a thick layer on it dries to a translucent white finish that looks a lot like, well, that maybe you love painting just a bit too much. You can paint it on thinly for a clear thin varnish effect, although a regular water-based gloss varnish would be a better choice for this job. If you use it on its own the layers have to be painted on thinly.

What finish does it dry to?

It dries to a high gloss finish. And I mean high gloss.

Do I brush it on or what?

Yes, you can brush it on for thin layers, but I find the textural qualities of the paint work well with good old kitchen spatulas, spoons, palette knives and pieces of strong cardboard. Use all of the above to spread it around and scratch and scrape into it. Have some fun!

How long does it take to dry?

Really thick layers can take a few hours to dry completely, but thinner layers are usually dry in an hour or so.

How do you clean up after using gel medium?

Just use warm water and soap as you would with acrylic paints.

Once you get the hang of it you'll more or less know what to expect from gel medium before it dries, but even then you can be in for a nasty or pleasant surprise. While experimenting for the following projects I did one and wasn't all that happy with it so I had a minor huffy and went to bed. Lo and behold in the morning the dried transparent colors looked much better than I had expected, confirming that old adage that mistakes sometimes work out for the best. And if you don't believe me, you can ask my adoptive parents.

SEE WHAT I MEAN?

OTHER MEDIUMS AND THEIR USES

I did mention that there are a wide variety of mediums available. Here are some of the more popular ones and their uses, but do check out your art store for more options because this is by no means a complete list. The names of individual products can also vary between brands.

IMPASTO MEDIUM—when you want opaque texture, impasto medium is what you should be buying. You just add it to paint and for some strange but wonderful reason it makes it thick without changing the color.

RETARDER MEDIUM—if you're having trouble with acrylic paint drying too quickly then this is what you need. Like the name says, it slows drying and gives you more time to manipulate the paint.

PAINTING MEDIUM—is used instead of water to dilute paint. When you add water to paint to thin it out you can lose some of the intensity of the pigment. Painting medium allows the paint to be thinned without changing the color. Pretty neat, huh?

MODELING COMPOUND/PASTE—I have been asked if you can use plaster on a canvas. The answer is no, because it cracks and falls off. But if you want very heavy-looking textural effects, modeling compound is the go. It's got a plaster-like finish that dries white. You can either add paint to it or paint over it after you've finished. Be warned that if you decide to mix paint in first you're going to need a mountain of paint because the compound is so thick. Best just to paint over it after it has dried.

CRACKLING MEDIUM—this is used to create a weathered and cracked appearance. Although methods vary between brands, you basically paint your canvas one color, paint over a layer of crackling medium, then apply another layer over the top. The crackling medium causes the top layer of color to split and crack, allowing the first layer of color to show through. Some may say that this cracked appearance looks quaint and rustic, but I say it just looks bloody awful. Sorry guys, but I just can't get into this one.

FLOW MEDIUM—allows you to really thin down the paint but maintain the color and opacity. This product can make paint so thin that you could use the result in an airbrush if you wanted to.

MATTE MEDIUM—although acrylics dry to a semi-matte finish, you might be the ultra matte type and you can use this to remove any trace of sheen from the paint. Either mix it in with the paint or apply as a final varnish. I once used this to tone down the shine of a final gloss varnish layer and was surprised just how effective it was—the glossy shine was almost completely eradicated.

GLOSS MEDIUM—one of the staples in the book, you can either add it to the paint or use it as a final layer to increase gloss and color depth. A real winner if you ask me.

PROJECTS

Although working with gel is really interesting, many of you will be tempted to overwork these projects because the gel and acrylic paint mixtures look so atrocious before drying. Patience is a virtue and you'll need it for these gel projects. However, if your virtue has long since vanished then go out for a few hours. Sometimes you've just got to get out of the way and let artwork do its thing.

WHERE DO I SIGN?

You may have noticed that all the examples in this book have one thing in common—there's no signature on any of them. And it isn't my lack of vanity, it's because I simply forgot. But it also goes to show that you don't have to sign your work if you don't want to. It's not a requirement or anything. But if you do, consider the following:

1. One valid reason to sign a painting is that if some day your work is worth a fortune a signature will help authenticate it long after you've fallen off the perch.

2. The traditional area to sign is the bottom over towards one of the corners, but you could always sign on the side of the painting if you think a signature would be too intrusive on the front. In fact, you could even just sign on the back of the painting in order to keep the front all nice and clean.

3. A fine round synthetic brush, about a size 1–3, is good for the fine lines of a signature. Just dip it in the paint and sign away, taking it slower than you would if you were using a pen.

4. Consider scratching your signature into the surface of wet paint. The end of a small brush can be good for this, or simply use a toothpick.

5. You don't always have to use all the letters in your name. Take a leaf from Zorro and use a single letter or pretend you're Prince and come up with a symbol. One customer from the shop duplicates a section from one of his tattoos to sign his work.

6. I have seen people use a fingerprint as a signature, but to me it always looks like some sort of painting mishap. Still, it might be your thing, so I thought I'd mention it anyway.

7. Whatever signature style you use, try and keep it somewhat discreet and in keeping with the colors of the work itself, otherwise it will look like some badly forged signature that was applied by an underpaid youth in an art sweatshop.

8. Even if you're not up for adding a signature, try and put a date somewhere on the back. Who knows, maybe one day you'll have so many paintings that you won't be able to remember exactly when you did them.

PROJECT 1

3-COLOR GEL

I'd spent ages experimenting with a range of colors and techniques when I finally came up with the prototype for this project. When one of my roommates arrived home (the one that actually does her dishes and takes out the bins) I immediately asked for her opinion. She paused. She looked, she gave me that "I'm not into it but I can't say that to him" look, before telling me that she "liked other ones you've done better," which was very tactful of her. I have to say, it made me think twice about this project and if I should include it at all. So when I took it to show my publisher and editor I wasn't sure how they'd react. To my surprise they both really liked it and I remembered that at one stage I did too. Although I'm not bashing my roomie for being honest, I am bashing myself for not sticking with my original feelings. It's true, you really can't please all the people all of the time. So if you love something you've done, keep loving it even if other people don't agree.

Get this:

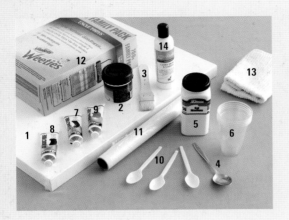

1. 24" x 36" pre-stretched canvas

2. 8 fl oz tester pot of beige acrylic paint

3. Medium sized flat brush

4. Dessertspoon

5. 17 fl oz pot of gel medium

6. 4 plastic cups

7. Tube of dioxazine purple acrylic paint

8. Tube of ivory black acrylic paint

9. Tube of raw sienna paint

10. 3 plastic spoons

11. Plastic wrap

12. Large empty breakfast cereal box

13. Cloth

14. Water-based gloss varnish

Step 1

Put down plenty of newspaper. Paint the canvas with two coats of beige paint. Allow it to dry between coats. Wash the brush. Using the dessertspoon, divide the gel medium evenly between three of the plastic cups. Add a tiny dab of purple, black and sienna paint to each cup. Mix each color with a clean plastic spoon until they are a pale pastel. Wrap the sienna/gel mixture with plastic wrap so it doesn't dry out.

Step 4

Turn the canvas to portrait and place a line of the raw sienna and gel medium mixture in the middle until it takes up about two-thirds of the canvas. Drag it with the cereal box as per Step 3. Allow the whole thing to dry completely.

Step 2

Spoon the contents of the purple and black gel medium mixtures in a line on to the top of the horizontal canvas. Keep spooning the mixture along the edge of the canvas until it is two-thirds along the top.

Step 3

Now, get the cereal box and place it in the paint/gel mixture at a 45 degree angle. Slowly drag a section of the mixture down the canvas. Don't worry if you run out of paint on the way down; these things work out for the best. Wipe the excess paint from the box with the cloth, then do the same thing to the remaining paint/gel. You may have to do a couple of drags to get all your paint down the canvas. Right now this artwork looks like a cartoon character that's been hit by a bus but the transparency will develop as you allow it to dry before moving to the next step. This may take a couple of hours.

Step 5

Pour some of the water-based varnish into the remaining cup. Dip the medium sized flat brush and paint on two coats of varnish, allowing time to dry between coats.

TIP

■ Try to use an artist quality purple paint like the dioxazine purple. The reason I say this is because I used a student quality purple paint in my prototype and although it was rich and transparent to begin with it faded to almost nothing after a few weeks.

PROJECT 2

BLACK MONOTONE

I think practically everyone goes through a stage where they have a thing for the color black. As a teenager growing up in a small country town I thought I looked particularly radical in my oversized black jumper and black jeans that I used to wear, even in the height of summer. I think they'd describe me as EMO now, but my father used to describe it as "walking around like the bloody village idiot." Anyway, I'll always remember strolling along in said outfit one day when a car drove past and some local yelled that I should "Go back to Sydney," which I thought was about the nicest thing that anyone had ever said to me. Well, now I do live in Sydney but the black gear is long gone. So when it came to choosing a color for this project I decided to revisit my old friend and make this monotone picture completely black. Using the glossy black finish of gel medium makes this project a study in texture. It may not show up in the photo, but this project has an architectural elegance to it that some will find striking and others will find drab. Black is like that. It can mean teenage angst, mature sophistication, understated elegance, unspoken terror, or mourning. To me, black is the most schizophrenic of all colors, which is why I think we all go through our black phase at some point. If you're not into it now, chances are you will be, you have been, or you will be again.

Get this:

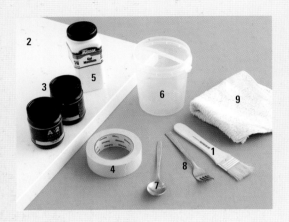

1. Medium sized flat brush

2. 24" x 48" pre-stretched canvas

3. 2 x 8 fl oz pots of ivory black acrylic paint

4. Masking tape

5. 17 fl oz pot of gel medium

6. Plastic bowl or container

7. Dessertspoon

8. Fork

9. Cloth

Step 1

Put down plenty of newspaper. Using the flat brush, paint the canvas with two coats of ivory black paint. Allow it to dry between coats. Place the masking tape down across the width of the painting so it forms an angle. Tear it off at the end with your fingers and press down firmly.

Step 4

Run the fork through the gel in horizontal lines. Then do the same vertically to create a cross-hatched pattern. The fork may get clogged with paint so give it a wipe with the cloth before getting back into it.

Step 2

Put the second pot of black paint and the entire contents of the gel medium into the plastic container. Mix thoroughly with the dessertspoon.

Step 3

Using the dessertspoon, slap the mixture onto the masked area and spread it out to an even, thick coating. Be careful not to go over the masking tape.

Step 5

Remove the masking tape while the paint is still wet and allow to dry. This is important because if you try to remove the tape when the gel mixture dries it practically tears the whole thing away.

INSPIRATION

The great Robert Smith of course!

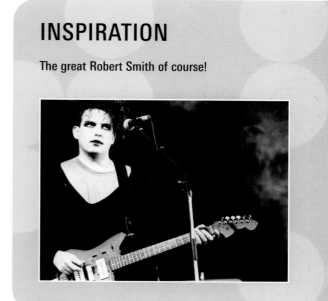

PROJECT 3

RED GEL

I've always had a thing for the color red. I think it goes back to when I was a kiddie growing up in Broken Hill on the edge of the desert in western New South Wales. The local famous artist was a chap named Pro Hart, who was known for his paintings of Australian landscapes featuring bold shades of red and orange. I can still remember seeing the first painting that really had an impact on me. It was a Pro Hart giant orange and red butterfly that used to hang in the foyer of the local civic center. I'm not sure if I liked it or not but the only other paintings I had seen before were lush landscape scenes of waterfalls with deer sitting languidly in the sunlight, a stark contrast to the dry, dusty environment around me. As for the deer, the only animals I saw lying languidly were the dead carcasses of emus and kangaroos on the side of the road. With this project, we're going to be doing multiple gel layers for a glaze effect. In some ways it's one of the more complicated projects in this book but don't let that put you off—it's still not hard to do. You will be surprised at just how effective these gel medium glazes can be in creating depth and increasing color intensity. This project does have a fair amount of waiting time as far as the drying of layers is concerned, but the end result really is worth it. As you will see, the whole painting has all the sheen and translucency usually associated with oil paintings. In fact, when I showed this to my friends, they all thought that it actually was an oil painting. Suckers!

Get this:

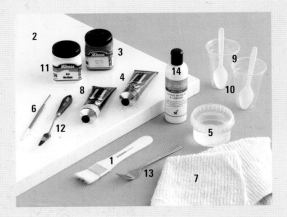

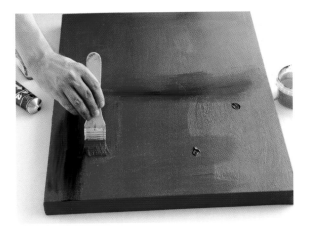

① Medium sized flat brush

② 18" x 24" pre-stretched canvas

③ 8 fl oz tub of brilliant alizarine (crimson) acrylic paint

④ Tube of carbon black acrylic paint

⑤ Plastic container filled with water

⑥ 1 smaller round bush. Get the cheapest you can— we're only going to use the handle anyway.

⑦ Two cloths

⑧ Tube of cadmium yellow light hue acrylic paint

⑨ 2 plastic cups

⑩ 2 plastic spoons

⑪ 8 fl oz tub of gel medium

⑫ Palette knife

⑬ Fork

⑭ Water-based gloss varnish

Step 1

Put plenty of newspaper down. Using the flat brush, paint the canvas with a rough coat of brilliant red (crimson) acrylic paint —remember to cover the sides as well. Allow it to dry. Wash the brush so it doesn't go all stiff. Apply a second coat of red, but only to half of the canvas. We're saving the other half for another technique. While the second coat is still wet, dab a few dots of black acrylic paint onto the surface. We're going to blend these two colors to create an interesting background surface. Now blend the two colors into each other. You may need to dip your brush into the plastic container filled with water to ensure the blending goes smoothly. Try and blend sections both horizontally and vertically to create an interesting contrast. Wash that brush again.

Step 2

While the blended paint is still wet, take the small round brush and turn it upside down. Now scratch the paint with the blunt end of the brush. Just scratch away randomly. Wipe the end of the brush with one of the cloths to remove excess paint that can accumulate between scratches.

Step 3

It's time to tackle the other half of the picture! Drop a glob of the cadmium yellow paint on the other half of the canvas and slap it about with the flat brush. Wait a few minutes before using one of the cloths to rub most of the yellow paint off. You will be left with a yellow stain. Leave to dry. Wash the brush again—and stop complaining about it!

Step 4

We can now start to apply the glazing layers. Use a plastic cup and one of the plastic spoons to mix a few scoops of gel medium with a tiny bit of yellow paint—about one part paint to ten parts gel medium. You can always add more layers later if need be.

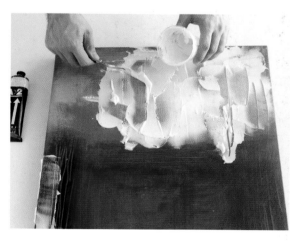

Step 5

Smear the gel/paint mixture onto the bottom section and the top right-hand corner of the canvas with the palette knife. Use the fork and make a few scratches. Be sure to limit all these shenanigans to the non-blended half of the painting.

Step 6

You will notice that your painting now has an awful pale yellow mess all over it. Even I was a bit worried about this when I first started with this technique. Don't fret too much because it will dry transparent. Put it out in the sun for a couple of hours and see what I mean. When the painting is dry, mix up some red paint gel medium as in Step 4. Apply this layer thickly and scratch it around a bit with the palette knife and fork like you did in Step 5. The resulting pink mush will dry to a clear red finish. Trust me! While you're waiting for it to dry wash one of the plastic cups.

Step 7

Although it doesn't show up so well in the pictures, you will find that the glazed areas are nice and glossy, but the unglazed sections are matte and the colors are a tad dull. Water-based gloss varnish to the rescue! Pour some into the clean plastic cup, and apply three coats using the trusty flat brush you used before. Allow it to dry between coats. Two is good, but three or four will make it really glossy. I must also admit that I also added a tiny (and I mean tiny) dot of ivory black paint to the bottom right hand corner and blended it with the varnish.

TIP

These two detail shots show how the scratching and glazing techniques reveal the layered colors. Although I have only done two glazed layers, you could easily go crazy and do as many as you like. Experiment and see what happens. Just remember to use the correct medium and you'll be set like a jelly. Hmmm ... not really sure that joke worked.

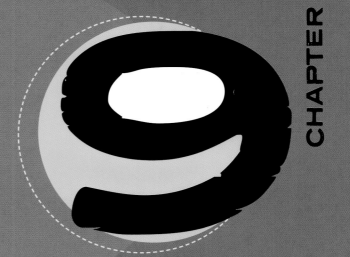

CHAPTER

Collage

Collage and I started off on the wrong foot. I was in my first yeat at high school, making a collage picture for our art class. I decided to include a very tame clipping of a topless woman in my composition, which I later found out was not the thing to do in a country Catholic school. So there I am, working away when the art teacher looks over my shoulder, grabs my picture, tears it up, gives me a good talking to and sends me to the chapel for detention! Not only that, but I also had to sort through the pile of old magazines and newspapers in the art room to ensure that no more lewd boobs were hiding in the pages to corrupt the minds of fellow students.

I wonder what Freud would make of all this?

But that's all behind us and now collage and I are the best of friends. It really is a lot of fun and easy to do. So what exactly is collage anyway? Basically, collage is a pattern or image built up from a range of materials. Most people will think of paper when they think of collage, but they're underestimating the incredibly wide range of materials that can fall under the collage banner. Virtually anything can be used for this medium. Wood, wire, carpet, fabric, plastic—you name it, if you can stick it together you can use it. Which brings me to the next feature of collage, the use of adhesives to put everything together. With the right adhesive, you can create a range of designs from flat, smooth images to highly textured and multi-dimensional projects. In fact, the word collage derives from the french verb "coller," which means "to stick." Ooh la la.

Although collage is often associated with bad school projects, it actually has a rather grand and esteemed history. Collage is largely thought to have been brought to the masses by Picasso and Braque and evolved during the Cubist movement of the early 1900s. People actually thought it was quite revolutionary at the time, as the use of paper—any type of paper— to create an artistic image was something that was considered quite daring. It's hard to imagine that the use of paper would create such a stir without the controversial content that frequently drums up publicity in today's art world.

Because the scope of collage is so wide, I'm going to have to limit it to the use of paper, but if you want to get carried away and introduce other materials then feel free to do so.

Although COLLAGE is often associated with bad school projects, it has a rather GRAND HISTORY.

MATERIALS

Paper

When you decide that collage is the go, you will need to have a collection of papers. Nothing is off limits here. Newspapers, decorative papers, regular lightweight cardboard, commercial packaging, old wrapping paper. If it's made of paper consider it a contender. The only thing that you may have to watch out for is the use of extremely fine papers, such as tissue paper. Because of the nature of adhesive, the fine qualities of tissue can be practically destroyed by use of a liquid glue. Still, that's not always a bad thing, as tissue paper and glue can be scrunched together for interesting textural effects. You'll see what I mean when we get to the projects.

ADHESIVES

The right adhesive makes a huge difference to the nature of your collage. Here are some of the choices:

PVA glue

DRYING TIME: They say 15–20 minutes, but I think you need about an hour or two. You may know this as woodworking glue. It has a water-based adhesive that dries clear and is usually diluted with water. It has been a staple item in collage for years. It is good, but I have found that if you try to layer more glue over a previously dried layer the moisture in the new layer tends to "reactivate" the dried glue. Although it's not bad to use I think you can do better.

Binder medium

DRYING TIME: About 5–15 minutes to become rather tacky and then another hour to dry completely. Can depend on the weather. On really hot days it starts to get tacky after just a few minutes, so you may have to work fast if you live in the boiling boondocks.

Binder medium is like the Holy Grail of adhesives to me. It's a water-based substance that is used to prepare and seal surfaces before painting with acrylics. It spreads easily and sticks like nobody's business. You can even use it as a final varnish for a semi-gloss finish. It also doesn't have the reactivation problem I've found in PVA. Because it's water based it can be easily cleaned up with soap and water. Although it's white in color it does dry to a clear finish, so don't panic when you first paint it on because those milky patches soon disappear.

Spray adhesive

DRYING TIME: More or less straight away, then a few hours to really become permanent. If you've ever stuck a piece of paper down with a glue and then found it rippled like crazy when it dried, spray adhesive is the good news you've been waiting for. It's like an aerosol can with glue inside and all you do is spray and stick. However, it is important to note that the fine mist of glue can also end up in your lungs if you're not careful. So always use a dust mask and spray in a well-ventilated area.

I've tried both expensive and cheaper spray adhesives and I have to report there is a difference. The cheaper ones generally don't stick all that well. They do the job, but the stuck items tend to peel at the corners, which is not quite the look you should be going for. I recommend 3M Multi-purpose. It is pricey but the results are superior. It really does maintain a strong bond. This is one time when parting with the extra bucks is worth it.

Spray adhesive is also good for fine papers like tissue, because it won't saturate the paper with water and you also get no rippling whatsoever. For this same reason it is also good to use with papers with colors that tend to run. The only thing you have to remember to do is to spray your papers from a distance of about 8"–12". If you spray too close you can get a concentration of adhesive that looks like a greasy stain on some papers. Unfortunately, it doesn't go away when the glue dries. Believe me, I thought it would and I ruined a really nice piece that now lives in my garage and makes me feel guilty every time I see it.

The adhesive in these cans is not water-soluble and will leave a grainy film on surfaces. You can remove it with lighter fluid on a cloth, but the best idea is to put down heaps of newspaper before you start. There I go again with my "prevention is better than cure" speech!

Gel medium

DRYING TIME: Up to a couple of hours if it's thin; if it's thick it will take longer. Also depends on how hard Mr Sun is shining.

There is a whole section (pages 98–99) devoted to this medium, but it also makes a good, thick adhesive for collage. Just remember that if you apply it too thickly (over about ⅟₁₆"–⅟₁₈") it leaves a milky film. Keep it thin and you'll be fine.

Multipurpose craft glue

DRYING TIME: Fixes in about 10–20 minutes but you need to leave it for a few hours for it to dry completely.

If you're planning on using any slightly heavy objects such as carpet pieces or plastic tubing you will need a good multipurpose craft glue. UHU All Purpose is a good choice. If you are going to use foam or plastics be sure that the glue you use is suitable. It will usually tell you on the pack. Some glues have a solvent base that can eat into these materials. Whatever you decide to use, always ensure that the glue you buy dries clear. You don't want any annoying milky patches on your collage.

OTHER COLLAGE EQUIPMENT

I just thought I'd give you a quick rundown of some of the equipment that I use in these projects.

Acrylic paints

You may need these to color the background of your piece. They can also be mixed with the binder medium to create light glazes. Flip back to Chapter 1 for more info.

Brushes

Cheap, flat hog hair brushes are the go here. Or get yourself some smaller house painting brushes to do the backgrounds with acrylic paint or to spread glue over larger sections of your collage. You may also need these if you decide to apply a final coating of varnish to your work. And speaking of final coats ...

Varnish

A water-based varnish can be used to add a certain type of finish to your work. Varnishes come in gloss, satin and matte versions. Not only do they seal your work, they also protect your collage against dust. A picture hung on a wall for a few months/years can get surprisingly dirty. At the risk of sounding like an advertisement from 1950, a couple of coats of varnish makes your collage a breeze to clean. Not only that, it seals your work and makes colors that much more vibrant. Thanks water-based varnish, you've saved my collage and my marriage!

Scissors

If you don't already have a good sharp pair then it's about time you did. It's not as if you won't use them for other things. Just pick some up at the supermarket next time you're there.

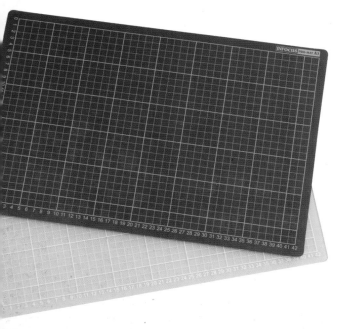

Cutting mat

A cutting mat is made from a flexible plastic material that is so dense you can't actually cut through it. While these are not an absolute necessity, it does make the job easier. It's great to use when cutting out shapes with a blade and will protect your table. They come in various sizes, but I find the most useful one is a Tabloid (11" x 17"). They usually come in green and white translucent versions. While the translucent ones look much more stylish I find they are more brittle and tend to crumble in areas with repeated cutting. This doesn't happen overnight but it is something to consider if you are planning to use your cutting mat regularly. But the translucent ones are good if you are going to use them over a lightbox, because they allow the light through whereas the green ones are completely opaque.

All things considered, I say stick with the green ones. They don't look as nice as the translucent ones but they are more durable. It does pay to be practical sometimes.

If your budget is tight, or you just forgot to buy a cutting mat, you can always use a kitchen chopping board or an old magazine. It's not the same but will do the job just as well.

Circle cutter

If you plan to collage with lots of circles, a circle cutter is the way to go. Sure, you can spend a lot of time cutting them out yourself but one of these gizmos makes the whole job easier and more accurate. A circle cutter basically looks like a compass with a small blade on one end. You just stick the point in your paper, extend the arm with blade to where you want it and move it around in a circle. It cuts a much neater shape than you (or should I say "I") could do by hand. Circle cutters range from cheap to expensive. I've tried them all and recommend you get a cheaper one unless you are planning to cut out

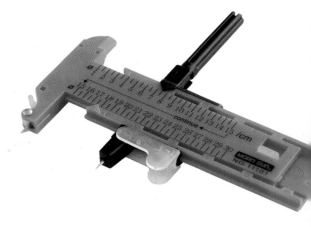

Real life weekend artist—profile 1

Richard Briggs is a friendly English guy who used to come into the store regularly. We got chatting one day and he showed me some of his work. I really liked his sketches of Sydney. He also mentioned that he was a full-time architect and did his drawings on the side, and was one of the first people I thought of when I decided to do profiles for this book.

Did you study art at University?
No I did architecture, but we were encouraged to use art as design generators. Apart from the regular course components you could do some art history or life drawing.

How did you start with the whole art thing?
I'm from England and I went traveling through a few countries on my way to Australia. I had a lot of time to really stop and think about my surroundings. I felt I was relying too much on my camera, so I just decided to sit down and draw what I could see. By the time I arrived in Sydney my head was full of ideas on how to draw and paint my new surroundings. Eventually, I realized I had to start working again, but I thought to myself that I can't let this spirit for drawing go because I've found something that I really, really enjoy. I really wanted to communicate that the city we live in can be beautiful, can be fantastic and can also be a bit ragged around the edges, but that's often where the interesting parts lie.

So when did you start to go commercial?
I used to run a market stall where I'd sell my drawings. It was fairly successful. There was a café next to the market and they wanted one of my works for their walls. It was then that I realized maybe I could take this whole art thing further. I approached a couple of cafés and organized a couple of exhibitions. I didn't sell much, but it was all about exposure and just plain fun.

I had started to get my sketches printed to a larger scale. One day a well-known gallery owner happened to be at the same printer I use and remarked to the staff that he liked my work. They passed this onto me and I approached him and I had my first gallery show.

After my first show I thought that I could form a path out of this, maybe not financially, but in doing what I want to do. I now want to take it to the next level.

When do you do your work?
Mainly weekends. It takes me a while to get into things. I can't really draw at night because I've been working all day.

Have you got a basic philosophy?
I think you've got to take every opportunity that knocks on your door with both hands, otherwise you will regret it and you won't get to where you want to be.

Everybody knows this is nowhere 2007

millions of circles. They all work pretty much the same, but the expensive ones are usually sturdier and the blades are sharper. Bear in mind that circle cutters can't cut circles to an infinite size—the cutter will only extend so far, so make sure it extends to the size you need. They usually state the maximum circle diameter on the pack.

PROJECTS

The projects I've devised are pretty simple to do, but I've thrown in a couple of more difficult ones for all you adventurous types out there. This section was a lot of fun for me and contains a couple of personal favorites. The one good thing about collage is that it makes you think about materials in a different way. That newspaper in the recycling bin suddenly has possibilities. That piece of wrapping paper isn't just for wrapping presents and those old pieces of cardboard could become something special. Part of being creative is seeing things in a different way, so take the time to look around and see what you could use. Although I'm not one for platitudes, I do love the saying that "One man's trash is another man's treasure." When it comes to collage that can literally be the case.

IT'S OKAY, BUT ...

Once you've created an artwork you like, you will inevitably want to show it to other people to see what they think. This can be a good and a bad thing, because there will almost certainly be someone who doesn't respond quite as enthusiastically as you'd like. It's hard not to take half-smiled responses and furrowed brows personally, but don't let these things put you off too much. As much as people like to think they have that fashionable "I don't care what other people think" approach—I think most people do care, it's just that the more confident ones continue with what they're doing regardless.

You also have to bear in mind that the most people won't like something unless they've been told that they should. If it hasn't been in some glossy magazine or newspaper supplement they won't know what to make of it. And don't feel that because you didn't pay sackfuls of cash for your art that it has no value. If you like it then it should stay on your wall, no matter what anyone else thinks. Like I always say, it doesn't matter if it's good taste, it doesn't matter if it's bad taste, just so long as it's your taste.

PROJECT 1

PEBBLES

This collage project is simple, clean, harmonious and all those other things that interior design magazines go on about. It also illustrates my point that collage isn't always about excessive glue and paper. Although I've chosen natural colors to fit in with the organic shapes, don't let that stop you from taking the opposite approach and using vivid colors for a completely different look. Copy me if you like but see if you can put your own stamp on it as well. Many of you won't have cut shapes out of paper since you used plastic scissors and picked your nose when people were actually looking, so my one tip is take it slowly (the cutting not the picking) so your shapes will have a smooth, even curve. And if you don't then you'll have to pick up rubbish in the playground at lunchtime.

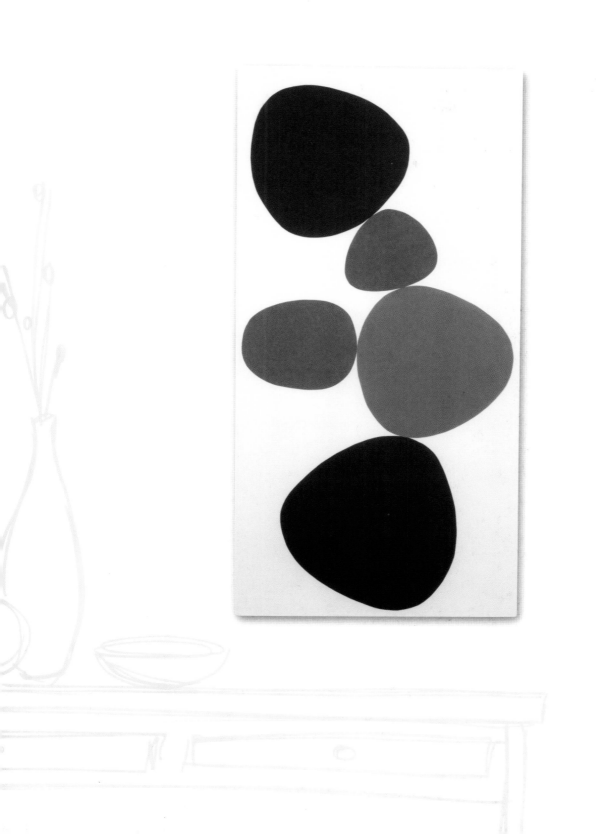

Get this:

1. 15" x 30" pre-stretched canvas

2. House painting brush

3. 8 fl oz tester pot of light beige house paint

4. Photocopied pebble templates (See Templates, pages 220–221)

5. Scissors

6. Colored papers in both Letter & Tabloid sizes. I've used two shades of blue and a bronze color in metallic finishes.

7. HB pencil

8. Eraser

9. Spray adhesive

10. Dust mask

11. Cloth

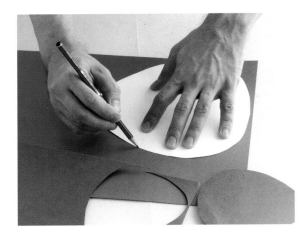

Step 1

Put down plenty of newspaper. Using the brush, give the canvas two coats of beige paint. Allow it to dry between coats. Photocopy templates and cut out with scissors. (See details on pages 220–221 for sizing to Tabloid if you need larger pebbles like the ones I've used here.) Using the pencil, trace around the templates on colored paper. Cut out the shapes. Use the eraser to rub off any pencil marks that remain.

Step 3

When you're happy, spray the back of each pebble with spray adhesive (outdoors with plenty of newspaper and ideally wearing a dust mask). Make sure you give it a good coat of glue.

Step 2

Play with arrangement of the pebbles on your canvas.

Step 4

Stick the pebble to the canvas. Press down with the cloth.

TIP

■ Are you stumped when it comes to choosing the color of your paper pebbles? Don't forget the 3-color rule isn't just for paint. You can apply it to your paper selections as well.

Variation To change the whole look you could cut some additional shapes and place them on top of each other. It kind of reminds me of butterfly wings or peacock feathers.

PROJECT 2

STREET POSTERS

I really like walking around the city, particularly the inner-city areas. I know it's dirty, I know there are crazy people about and I know some people just don't feel safe but for some reason I just feel right at home. I particularly like the layers of street posters that go up on walls and building site facades. There's a telegraph pole just outside the art store and every Saturday, without fail, I see some kid wrapping event posters around it, only to have them ripped down by a fluro-clad council-worker about two hours later. I rather like some of those posters and have been known to go and rip them down to keep for myself before the council workers arrive. I think walls of aged posters are almost like time machines, with poster after poster and event after event pasted up for all to see. It's kind of like some form of paleography (get out your dictionary). So I thought why not bring the filthy outdoors indoors? This is also a project in which you can go nuts. If you don't like what you've done, then rip it off or glue something else over the top. Mistakes are part of the plan. For a project like this, less is not as effective as more, and shoddy is a good thing.

Get this:

1. Binder medium

2. 36" x 48" pre-stretched canvas

3. Medium sized flat brush

4. 5 large sheets of tissue paper

5. 8 fl oz pot of neutral gray acrylic paint

6. Multiple copies of those free street music magazines See Tips for ... er ... tips on this.

7. Scissors

Step 1

Squirt the binder medium directly onto the canvas and spread it around with the flat brush. Place the tissue paper over the binder medium. Scrunch it around to create a bit of texture. Allow it to dry. Wash the brush.

Step 3

Rip a few copies of adverts you like out of the street music magazines. Try and get about 2–4 copies of each advert. Trim them with scissors if need be, but keep it rough. Now pour more of the binder medium on the canvas, and spread it out with our trusty flat brush and place the advertisements down. Work quickly now!

Step 2

Use the flat brush again to paint over the whole canvas with a coat of neutral gray acrylic. Be rough about it —it doesn't matter if it looks a little patchy. Allow it to dry thoroughly. Wash the brush again.

Variation You could always paint a few patches like I did here with a tube of cobalt blue hue acrylic.

Step 4

Rip the corners of the posters or overlap them if you want. For a weathered look, let the binder dry for a few minutes and rip sections of the poster away. It's all about street cred and that means looking rough around the edges—or at least pretending to (if you live in Sydney).

TIPS

■ Don't have access to street—gig magazines? Buy a music magazine instead and photocopy the pages you like. Color photocopies can be expensive so just do them black and white.

■ Street posters tend to be stuck down in rows, so try to have a couple of grouped sections to mimic the young-hoodlum technique.

PROJECT 3

TISSUE TRIO

Remember at the beginning of this chapter when I said that you should be careful when using tissue paper because it can be destroyed when used with a liquid adhesive? Well, in this project we're using that potential problem and making it a feature. The layers of tissue do indeed become transparent and that's a good thing; you get a three-dimensional effect because the colors of all the tissue become apparent. Up until now I've recommended you use a paint-on, water-based gloss varnish. And although I still think it's great, for this project we're going to have to use a spray varnish instead. I found that the dyes used to color the tissue are water based and when you brush over the tissue with a water-based gloss it runs and stains like crazy. But when you use a spray gloss varnish you minimize this problem. If there's a will there's a way, and there's usually a product as well.

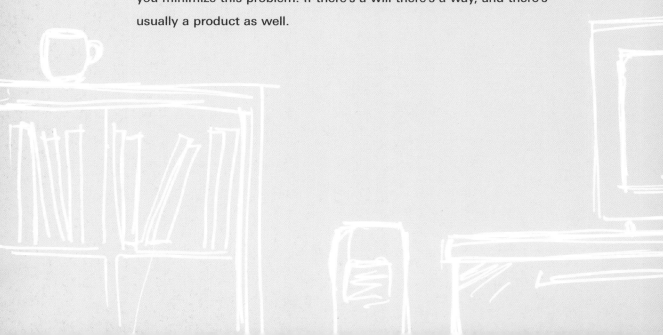

Get this:

1. Medium sized flat brush

2. 15" x 36" pre-stretched canvas

3. 8 fl oz tester pot of beige paint

4. Scissors

5. 3 packets of colored tissue paper

6. Binder medium

7. Dust mask

8. Spray gloss varnish

Step 1

Put down plenty of newspaper. Using the flat brush, paint the canvas with two coats of beige paint. Allow it to dry between coats. Clean the brush and let that dry as well. Use the scissors to cut out three largish oblongs of each of the three colored tissue papers. (I cut a half a sheet from my packets that was about 14" x 19".)

Step 3

Squirt on more of the binder medium and brush over the first layer of tissue and about another 20 percent of the remaining area. Apply the second piece of tissue and pat like before. Allow it to dry and wash the brush again. Repeat this overlapping process with the final piece of tissue paper, leaving a section of the canvas binder and tissue paper free. Allow it to dry.

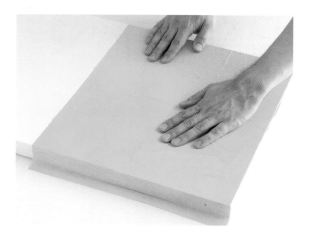

Step 2

Squirt some binder medium directly onto the canvas. Using the flat brush spread it over about one third of the canvas, including the sides. Take the first tissue paper layer and place it down on the binder medium and PAT it down gently with your hands. As you do this you will see the tissue becoming slightly transparent. Allow it to dry then wash your brush.

Step 4

Rip any excess tissue paper from the sides. Take the whole thing outside, put down more newspaper and pop on the dust mask before applying a light layer of spray gloss varnish. Allow to dry before applying another two coats.

TIPS

- Need help picking your tissue paper colors? Is that a bird? Is that a plane? No, it's the trusty 3-color rule coming to the rescue yet again!

- You may notice that the dye in the tissue can start to run into the binder medium as you are brushing away. This is no big deal because you are going to stick another layer of tissue over it anyway. But do be careful not to spread any stained binder onto the last section of the canvas. We don't want it looking all messy. If you do just touch it up with a slap of paint, although I found I needed to do 2–3 coats to cover the stain.

- When you apply the layers of spray varnish keep the coats light. If you saturate the surface with one superthick coat the color in the tissue paper will begin to bleed.

- If you rubbed a whopping hole in your artwork (so easy to do) just keep going and patch it up with a smaller piece of tissue later. Use another color so it doesn't look like you're trying to cover a mistake. If the mistake is relatively minor, just leave it alone.

PROJECT 4

ORIENTAL CIRCLE

I think I got the idea for this project from hanging around Sydney's Chinatown. Just lately I've been there quite a bit for food, but I always make the time to have a look at those stores with names like "Ballpoint Luck Plenty" and "Cute Play Now Friends." They really do have the most amazing array of pens and stationery items, and the designs intrigue me in that they can be minimalist, childlike and traditional all in one go. The art store also has a range of Japanese printed papers that customers often buy for wrapping paper. While I'm sure they make for very stylish gifts, I wanted to come up with a project that made use of these unique Asian designs in a minimalist but fun way. And if the truth be known, I was also just like looking for an excuse to use my circle cutter! Really do love that gadget …

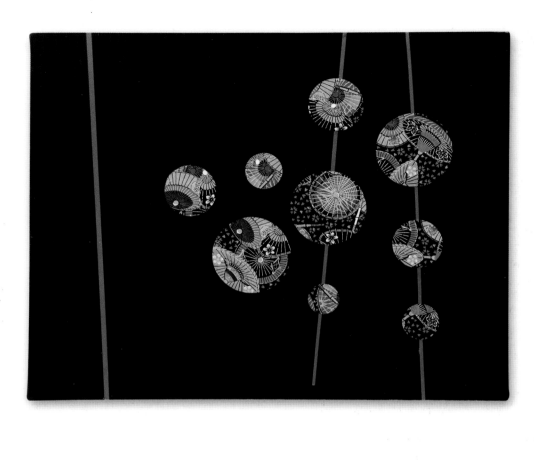

Get this:

1. Medium sized flat brush

2. 16" x 20" pre-stretched canvas

3. 8 fl oz pot of ivory black acrylic paint

4. Scissors

5. Tabloid sheet of red paper/light cardboard

6. Ruler

7. HB pencil

8. Circle cutter

9. Cutting mat (or use an old magazine)

10. A couple of sheets of Asian print paper around Letter size

11. Binder medium

12. Plastic cup

13. Water-based gloss varnish

Step 1

Put down plenty of newspaper. Using the flat brush, paint the canvas with two coats of ivory black paint. Allow it to dry between coats. Clean the brush. Use the scissors to cut a selection of paper strips from the red paper. I made mine about ¼" wide—but firstly I drew a line with the ruler and HB pencil to ensure the measurements were accurate.

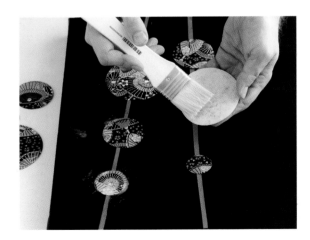

Step 3

Play with the arrangement of your circles and red lines on the canvas. When you're happy, remove the pieces of paper. Apply a slap of binder medium with the flat brush and press the paper pieces into place again. Wash the brush again. Allow the whole thing to dry for a couple of hours.

Step 2

And now for a spot of circle cutting madness. Use your circle cutter on the cutting mat to cut a selection of circles of different sizes from the Asian print paper. Use my picture for size inspiration, or just do what you think is best.

Step 4

Pour some water-based gloss varnish into the plastic cup and use the flat brush to apply two coats of varnish over the whole artwork including the paper sections, allowing time to dry between coats.

TIPS

- No circle cutter? You can always use scissors to cut out outlines made from cans, cups and jars. Take it slowly with the cutting so you get a clean curve as opposed to a circle that looks like it was trimmed with toenail clippers.

- It may seem odd, but don't hesitate when you apply the varnish to the paper. The colors of the paper will most likely darken slightly but it will look good in the end.

- Asian print papers can be found in art stores, but if that's not an option you could just as easily use printed wrapping papers. They don't have to be Asian prints. Think outside the circle if need be. Keep this design minimal. Think "zen, zen, zen," not "how can I fit 400 circles on one medium-sized canvas?" Actually, that might look kinda good. Disregard that last comment.

10

Street art:
why should petty criminals have all the fun?

So what exactly is street art? Well, it's basically anything you see on the street that gives the authorities grief. Graffiti, in its various forms, is street art. Stenciling and spray painting are in this category as well, and as much as I hate them, those ubiquitous tags are street art too.

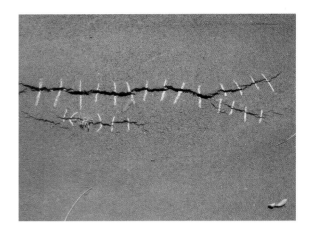

But make no mistake—writing on public surfaces is illegal. Stenciling designs on public walls is against the law. The authorities spend millions removing graffiti and trying to prevent its return. It is regarded by some as an example of a complete lack of respect for society and is an offence punishable under the law.

Now that I've got all that out of the way, I just have to say that I do have a soft spot for some forms of street art. Notice that I said some, not all. Like many commuters, I too have looked out of train windows and tut-tutted at the sheer volume of tags that appear along railway tunnels and factory walls. Just in case you don't know, a tag is a stylized signature of an artist created with paint or permanent markers. If you live in a place where there are teenagers, you've almost certainly seen these. They are a relatively recent phenomenon and their origins go back to 1960s New York. I'm sure the people who make these tags get an enormous thrill out of doing so, but it's just the number of them and their

before

after (sigh)

I'm going to encourage you to try **STREET ART** on canvas in your own **HOME.**

similarity that make my eyes roll. I also feel sorry for small business owners whose exterior walls look like some bad patchwork quilt, because they have to keep covering up graffiti with paint that doesn't quite match the original.

But every now and then I see a piece of graffiti that catches my eye in a good way. When I first came to Sydney, the bus I caught used to go past a wall on which someone had written in huge letters "I LOVE YOU—YES YOU!" I always wondered whom that message was for as I looked around that bus and noticed that all the other passengers, like myself, were smiling. There is also someone who went through a phase of spray painting waving aliens on walls near my house. I was actually a bit sad when I saw one such alien being blasted away with a high-pressure water gun. And I still think fondly of the person who drew chalk "stitches" on cracked pavements on my way to work.

But I know you can't have it both ways. One man's art is another man's eyesore and another graffiti remover's problem. So, just so you know, I'm going to encourage you to try street art on canvas in your own home. Hey, maybe I should have called it home art instead!

You know, sometimes I am just so uncool.

MARKERS—THEY'RE NOT JUST FOR THE BACK OF BUS SEATS

It's a familiar sight in the store. Two teenagers with caps (why is it always caps?) walk into the store and ask "Do you sell solids?" (Solids being markers filled with solidified paint, and highly valued by the graffiti set.) The answer is a definite 'No' accompanied with an I'm-keeping-my-eye-on-you-so-don't-even-think-about-pinching-anything-cos-we'll-bust-you-from-here-to-the-moon look. They then ask about spray paints before asking again about the paint markers. I have to say that not all are like this, some actually do buy things. There were two graffiti types that used to come in regularly for a while. They were nice enough guys and worked as apprentice electricians by day and vigilante graffiti artists by night (which meant that they were BREAKING THE LAW, don't forget). One day I asked them why, if they were so interested in painting, they didn't enroll in art school. I mean, they were obviously willing to put the time in and probably risked life and limb doing their thing. One told me that it was his thing and he "didn't want to be told what to do" and the other one said that "if it was legal it wouldn't be as much fun." I guess that pretty much sums it up. Still, I think it is a shame that they had all this talent and creative interest that would probably just disappear once they grew out of their graffiti stage.

So, just because markers are associated with pimply cap-wearers, don't think that they're not for you. Don't worry, I'm not going to ask you to get up at 2 am to dangle by your toes from a railway carriage to create your own tag. What I am going to do is show you that markers can be used on canvas to create some interesting effects. And don't worry if you can't draw because in some of the projects we'll be using rulers and stencils.

MARKERS—NOW YOU HAVE MORE OPTIONS

All markers aren't created equal. You can't just go and pick up a packet of cheap markers with the expectation that they'll do the job. But the good news is you can use ordinary permanent markers that you can buy in almost any supermarket and newsstand. If you need a larger range of colors then you're going to have to get hold of paint markers, which are usually stocked by most art stores.

Although there are a multitude of markers out there we are going to be dealing with one of two types:

1) Permanent markers

The name says it all. Once on, these babies don't come off in a hurry. They are usually lightfast as well, although I have noticed that they do tend to fade slightly and black colors can take on a brownish tinge. Those markers that you've used in the office that are black, green, red or navy in color are in this category.

2) Paint markers

Graffiti kids all over will know what these are about. As the name says, these are full of paint, rather than ink, as opacity is important. The tip size can also vary and the general rule is the larger the tip the better. The best thing about paint markers is that they come in a variety of colors, including metallics. They are also fade and weatherproof. I guess there's no point writing something on a building if people on the train can't give it a bored glance before checking their watches and wondering why this train is always so late. Gotta keep those commuters enthralled come rain, hail or shine!

PERMANENT MARKERS ... or are they?

Although they are called permanent markers there are ways to remove them if you happen to get carried away and end up with marker all over your table. What you need is a can of hairspray. Just spray it on the marker lines and wipe off with a dry cloth. I've tested this out on a number of surfaces around my house and it worked amazingly well on any glass, plastic or painted surface. Unfortunately, if you make a mistake on your painted canvas I have found that hairspray will remove some, but not the entire color. It's also not quite as effective on porous surfaces such as unsealed timber, but even then it removes a lot of the marker ink.

I'm not sure how this will affect all surfaces, so you might want to test it first in a discreet area to ensure that nothing is going to get damaged.

Tips

The tip or nib is the point at the end of the marker that distributes the ink or paint. I know that seems a ridiculously obvious thing to say, but you have to remember that someone out there will just have learnt something they didn't know. Markers basically come with two types of tips. These are:

1) **CHISEL TIPS**—have squarish shaped flat tip at an angle. Most tags are done with these because they are good for creating curved lines that vary in width. Due to their size they are also good for filling in large areas quickly.

2) **BULLET TIPS**—good for outlines, using with stencils and for filling in small areas.

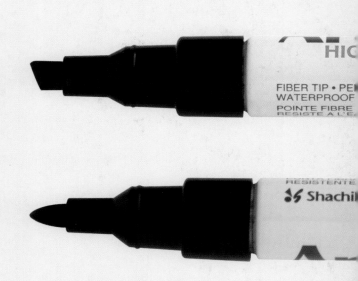

THE TYPE OF MARKERS/PENS YOU SHOULDN'T USE (Well You Can, But I Wouldn't If I Was You)

FLURO/HIGHLIGHTER PENS: These fade like crazy and are too transparent. You just won't see them if you put them over a colored background.

PACKETS OF CHEAP MARKERS LIKE YOU HAD IN PRIMARY SCHOOL: Bad tips and transparent ink = a big waste of money no matter how cheap they are.

OIL PAINT BARS: These are often confused for solid markers, particularly if you are a frustrated graffiti artist who has just been told by a sales assistant that they have no solid paint markers for sale and are determined to walk out of that art store with something in your pocket (whether you bought it or not). Basically, they are oil paint in a solid form—kinda like a big crayon made out of oil paint. They have their place but not for what we're trying to achieve here.

FINE FELT-TIPPED PENS: As we will be using markers on canvas these sort of fine-tip pens shred easily, because of the rough nature of the canvas/acrylic paint surface. They also tend to run out of ink because they really are only designed for small-scale use on paper. Put it this way, I've never busted any graffiti kids trying to steal these. Even petty crims know they're not right for the job.

REGULAR BALL-POINT PENS: Now you're just being silly.

MARKER TIPS

1) Put a lid on it

Remember when you were little you would leave the lid off your markers only to find that they didn't work the next day? Well, nothing's changed as you still have to put the lids back on. This is particularly the case with paint markers because the paint dries in the tip and then you're back to square one.

2) Shake it with the lid on it

Paint markers also need to be shaken to ensure that the contents blend so you get a strong, opaque color. When shaking your pen you must also remember to leave the lid on. I know this because I was demonstrating a marker to a lady and shook it vigorously with the lid off only to look up and see a line of marker paint down the front of her dress. I really didn't know what to say—luckily she was a sport about it and we didn't end up with an ugly consumer-affairs scene. What was that saying about a wise man learning from his own mistakes and an even wiser man learning from the mistakes of others?

3) In the beginning

When you first get your paint marker you can't just rip the lid off and start marking away like you can with a regular marker. You usually have to give it a good shake (with the lid on, of course) and then push the tip down on some paper a few times until the paint feeds into the fibrous tip. Sometimes you have to press the tip down quite a few times. It's annoying, but be patient in the knowledge that the paint, like Christmas, will eventually arrive. Be sure to also make a few lines and scribbles on a spare piece of paper until the paint is flowing consistently before you aim at your canvas.

4) Be an air head

Although markers aren't crazily toxic unless you practically snort or drink the contents, it is best to use them in a well-ventilated area to avoid breathing in the fumes. You don't have to set yourself up in a wind tunnel but do have a few windows open nearby.

PROJECTS

Sorry guys, but I won't be showing you the technique to do a good-looking tag. I'm afraid you'll have to ask someone less antique than myself for that sort of thing. But what I have come up with is a few projects that are quick to do and use techniques that assume you're not a seasoned graffiti fiend. In fact, if the idea of even using a marker on canvas seems foreign to you (it did to me when I started) then these are projects with non-intimidating baby steps.

On your markers ... get set ...

(I've been busting to use that dreadful pun ever since I started writing this chapter!)

PROJECT 1

SCRIBBLE BLOCK

I'm sure most of you don't remember the drawings you did as a child but somewhere in a box at your mum and dad's is a fine example of scribbling, and that's exactly what you have to do in this project. Yes, I want you to get ready to scribble your little heart out like you did as a kiddie on the dining room wall when mum wasn't looking. The good thing about scribbling is that there's really no right or wrong way to do it. Nobody can bust you on technique for this one. Another interesting thing about this project is that we are going to frame our work but not in the traditional sense. We're going to limit the size of the image on the canvas and leave a lot of nice white space to form a frame of its own. We're also going to use gloss varnish to add sheen to the painted area to further enhance our faux frame effect. The moral of this project is that you don't have to cover the whole canvas in color. Sometimes what you don't paint is just as important as what you do.

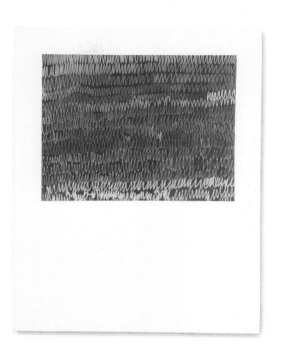

Get this:

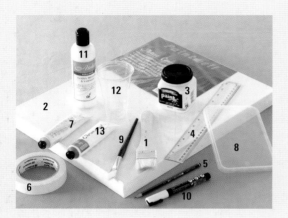

1. Medium sized flat brush

2. Two 14" x 18" pre-stretched canvases

3. 8 fl oz pot of white acrylic paint

4. Ruler

5. HB pencil

6. Masking tape

7. 2½ fl oz tube of lime green acrylic paint

8. Takeout container lid

9. ¾" flat synthetic brush

10. White medium sized bullet point paint marker

11. Water-based gloss varnish

12. Plastic cup

13. 2½ fl oz tube of magenta acrylic paint

Step 1

Using the flat brush, paint the canvas with two coats of white acrylic paint. Allow it to dry betwen coats. Using the ruler, make a couple of small marks with the HB pencil 1½" from the top and sides of the canvas and 8" from the bottom. Place masking tape along the outside of this oblong, and tear off at the ends.

Step 4

Pour a small amount of gloss varnish into the plastic cup. Dip the synthetic brush in then apply one coat over the colored area. Leave the white area unvarnished. Allow it to dry.

Step 2

Squeeze a good blob of the lime green acrylic paint onto the container lid and, using the synthetic brush, paint one coat on the inside of the masked area. Allow it to dry before doing another coat. Don't worry if it dries to a slightly patchy finish, but do try to cover up any pencil lines. Keep the tape in place because we're not done yet. Wash the brush clean.

Step 3

And now for the fun part. Get the white paint marker and scribble all over the lime green square. When you've had your fill of scribble action put it aside and allow to dry. Don't take that tape off.

Step 5

Remove the masking tape slowly to reveal your rather impressive glossy rectangle of an artwork. Remove any visible pencil marks with a bit of white paint. Repeat the whole process on a new canvas using the magenta paint instead of lime.

TIP

■ I scribbled a whole heap of small curly swirls but you can do whatever you like. Go larger or straighter, but make sure you leave some of the color showing through. You might even like to try different types of scribble if you decide to do more than one painting. I used a curly one for the lime painting and an up and down technique for the magenta.

PROJECT 2

DRAW ME A LINE

I don't think people really think of rulers and straight lines as being an art technique. Somehow, the thought of expressing yourself by splashing paint all around seems so much more in keeping with the "mad genius" concept of an artist. This is an ideal project for those of you who prefer to know what they're doing and aren't comfortable using a lot of paint and aren't yet clinically insane. Just because you're doing something in a highly structured way doesn't mean it has less artistic value than something done from a more emotive angle. While it's true that some artists are nuts, there is a whole other school that values symmetry, balance and proportion.

Get this:

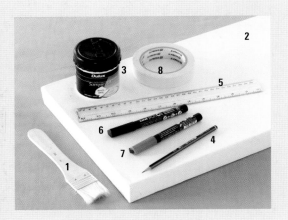

1. Medium sized flat brush

2. 12" x 24" pre-stretched canvas

3. 8 fl oz tester pot of aqua blue paint

4. HB pencil

5. 12" ruler

6. Black medium sized bullet point paint marker

7. Red medium sized bullet point paint marker

8. Masking tape

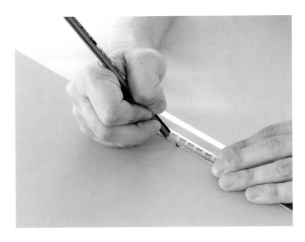

Step 1

Put down plenty of newspaper. Using the flat brush, paint the canvas with two coats of aqua blue paint. Allow it to dry between coats. Rinse the brush. Using the pencil and ruler, start marking points on the canvas at ¼" intervals on each of the opposing sides.

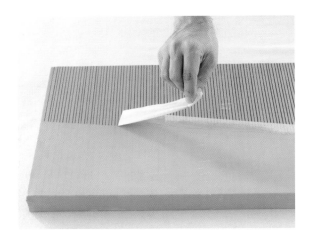

Step 4

Gently pull the tape off when the paint has dried.

Step 2

Now join the points alternating each line between the black and the red markers. I found it easier to do all the black lines and then go back and put in the red ones. Be careful that you don't accidentally put a black line where you should have put a red line.

Step 3

Apply the masking tape at an angle going the full length of the canvas. Tear it off at the end with your fingers and press down firmly. Then paint two coats of the aqua blue paint over the top section only. You may find the lines run and smudge but just keep painting — the second coat should cover this problem.

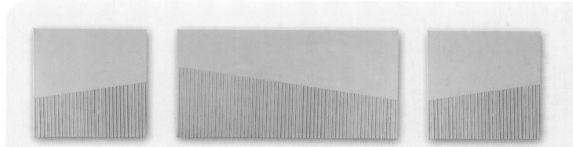

Variation Although I've done this project using a single slim canvas, you may want one that extends a little further. Rather than buy one filthy great long canvas, consider repeating the technique on a few smaller ones and hanging them next to each other. Just make sure they're the same height. We don't want to stuff up all that precise symmetry we've got happening.

PROJECT 3

RNA/DNA

I was always a fan of science at school and I think one of the reasons I liked it so much was not only did we get to muck around with the Bunsen Burners while the teacher wasn't looking, but I thought the illustrations in science textbooks were pretty cool as well. That's where the idea for this project came from. It sort of refers to every RNA or DNA ladder that I ever had to study. Initially, nobody liked this project, so I changed the color. It was originally a blue and white affair, but everyone slammed it so much that I changed it over to green and red giving it an entirely different feel. Which brings me to a point about color. Just because you don't like the color of something doesn't mean that you don't like the design of something. Almost everyone who looks at projects in this book will dismiss some of them purely on the basis of color. It's not easy, but try and see past the color and look at the shapes, or the technique that I've used. The big thing is experience. The more paintings you do and the more techniques you try the more you'll start to get over this very common form of color blindness.

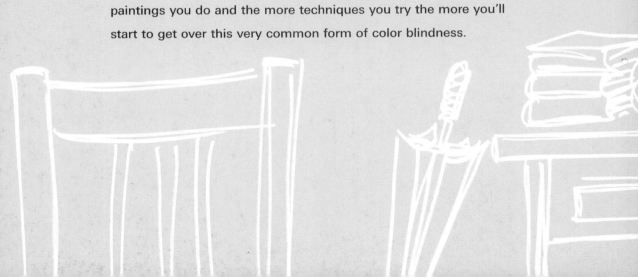

Get this:

1. Medium sized flat brush

2. 16" x 20" pre-stretched canvas

3. 8 fl oz tester pot of bright green paint

4. 12" ruler

5. Medium sized red bullet tip permanent marker

6. No. 5 round hog hair brush

7. Water-based gloss varnish

8. Plastic cup

9. Roll of red dot stickers. The ones I used were ½" wide.

Step 1

Put down plenty of newspaper. Using the flat brush, paint the canvas with two coats of bright green paint. Allow it to dry between coats and clean the brush. Using your ruler and red marker draw a series of zigzag lines, following the pattern in the main picture on page 159. If you make any mistakes touch them up with the No. 5 brush and green paint. Allow the paint lines to dry.

Step 3

Dip the No. 5 round brush in the gloss varnish and apply to the connecting points of the lines, then stick one of the dots onto the varnish. Press down firmly. Although the dots are adhesive they are not adhesive enough to stay in place by themselves. Allow to dry.

Step 2
Squirt some gloss varnish into the plastic cup.

TIPS

- It seems like overkill to use the gloss varnish to adhere the already sticky labels in place, but I can tell you that they will begin to peel after a couple of days and some will even fall off if you don't. I tried three different brands and the same thing happened every time. My favorite gloss varnish prevents this and seals them in place as well.

- Round dot label stickers are available in rolls from stationery stores and newsstands. They don't come in a rainbow of colors so you're probably going to be stuck with red, green white or yellow, if you're lucky.

- Be sure to lift the ruler off the canvas after you've drawn the lines. If you quickly slide it off you could be in for some annoying smudges.

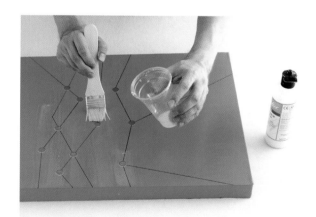

Step 4
Add more varnish to the cup and use the flat brush to apply two final coats to the entire surface of the artwork. Allow to dry between coats. You may find that the color of the lines bleeds slightly. Don't panic, the line is not going to dissolve before your very eyes. Just brush over any minor bleeding and you'll find it blends imperceptively into the varnish.

PROJECT 4

COW PARTY

If you think I haven't given enough guidance for this project then you're right. But what I have done is provided enough of an idea for you to do something on your own. Take the technique and run with it! Some of you will be able to get hold of a cow stencil like the one I used, but most of you won't. Just because I've used a cow stencil doesn't mean you have to. I want you to consider the possibilities of what type of stencils you can get your hands on. What about a firetruck, a teddy bear shape, or even a whale? Just head on down to the nearest craft section of your art store and see what you can find. They usually come in themed packs, so like me you might find yourself tossing up between the Barnyard Buddies and the Seabed Friends. Decisions, decisions! So why did I choose the cow? No reason. I just thought it was kind of cute.

Get this:

1. 24" x 30" pre-stretched canvas

2. 8 fl oz pot of white acrylic paint

3. Red medium sized bullet point permanent marker

4. Green medium sized bullet point permanent marker

5. Children's farmyard animals stencil. I used the cow.

6. Medium flat brush

Step 1

Put down plenty of newspaper. Using the flat brush, paint the canvas with two coats of white acrylic paint. Allow it to dry between coats. Decide on how you will pattern the canvas before you start stenciling. A quick sketch of how you would like the finished artwork to look is a good way to begin.

Step 3

When you get tired of doing red cows do a few green ones to break things up. Repeat until you're happy with the result.

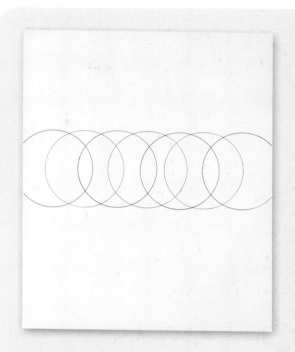

Step 2

Trace out one cow with the red marker. Be careful when you remove the stencil because some brands of markers will remain slightly wet and you'll smudge the lines if you just drag it off to the side. If you look closely at the picture on page 163 you'll notice this happened to me a few times, but I decided to leave it as I liked the furry effect it gave some of the shapes. The photographer liked it as well.

Variation Still can't get hold of a stencil? You could always just use a bread and butter plate like the one I used here.

TIPS

- Although the canvas is white, the two initial coats of acrylic white paint will give the final product a better finish and the surface is easier to draw on.

- Try to do each stencil in a single line without lifting your marker from the canvas. Lifting the marker tends to create uneven line widths in the shape and

can look a bit sloppy. Do some practice beforehand to get your technique down pat.

- Made a mistake? You can fix up mistakes with the acrylic paint. Dab paint over the area like you would correction fluid, let it dry then get back in the saddle and start again.

Stencils:
spray it, don't say it

Stenciling is all over the place these days. It may have started in the streets, but now it has also been adopted by the graphic design fraternity for use in advertisements aimed at the youth market. It's the street art you see in shop windows and on their outside walls. Regardless of its mainstream tendencies it continues to be popular among graffiti artists because it is so easy—all you have to do is cut a stencil and master the basic spraying technique and you're ready to go.

STENCIL DESIGNS

There are basically two types of stencil designs:

1) Silhouettes

2) Detailed images

Silhouettes are just basic outlines of an object filled in with solid color. While everything has an outline, not every outline is suitable for a stencil.

For example, both the stencil outlines on the right are from images of sharks, but as you can see the one on the top immediately looks like a fish, whereas the one below is not nearly as obvious; there are not enough details and the perspective is at the wrong angle. It takes practice to know what will work and what won't, but you do develop an eye pretty quickly. I've provided a few project templates for you to use at the back of this book (pages 218–219), but when you start to do your own you have to look out for outlines that actually look like the object you want to use. There are a few ways to do this:

● Trace around a picture of the object with a HB pencil and tracing paper. Hold the tracing paper up and see if the silhouette looks like the object. You can always ask a friend if you're not sure. If they don't know what it is there's a good chance no one else will either.

● Another method is to photocopy the image then cut out the object. Flip the cutout over and if you can still tell what it is then you can put it in the "Yes" pile.

● Sometimes if you squint your eyes you can see if the image will be suitable. You may even have to eliminate certain details to get the right effect.

Once you are comfortable with doing basic silhouettes consider doing more detailed stencils. These have more of the features of the object. There is more cutting out and time involved, but this can be very satisfying when you see the final result. All that slightly tedious cutting will be worth it in the end when you pull back that paint-soaked card to reveal your design in all its detailed glory.

Although making your own stencils measures highly on my Fun Richter Scale, you can also use existing objects as stencils. You can use almost anything for this purpose. If you like the shape then give it a go, and if you don't like the shape you should give it a go anyway; you just might surprise yourself. In the projects I devised for this chapter I've used both CDs and cheap lacey material to different effect.

OTHER THINGS YOU'LL NEED FOR STENCILING

In addition to a cutting mat (see page 122 for details on this) you will also need the following:

Stencil card

People who want to start stenciling often make the mistake of buying acetate sheets to create their stencil. Acetate is a thin, transparent plastic sheet—the type that was used in overhead projectors, when they were still around. While you can use this product, it falls down in a number of areas. Firstly, you can't draw on it with a pencil or run it through a photocopier (unless you buy a photocopier-friendly acetate). Secondly, the paint does not dry quickly on the stencil, so you have to wipe it off all the time if you're doing multiple sprays. Finally, it tends to become brittle and can crack with repeated use. It is also hard to cut out because the plastic puts up more resistance against the blade, particularly on circles and curved shapes.

With all that in mind, I say go the cardboard! Anywhere between 200–260 gsm will be just fine. This weight is thin enough to go through most photocopiers and printers, and is easy to cut as well. I have run up to 290 gsm through my trusty home inkjet printer and although it did work if I helped the paper feed, the printer made an awful lot of unhappy noises. Manila folders trimmed to fit into a Letter size are also a good option if you're really hard up for choice. It may seem light but trust me it will do the job. Whatever you do, don't use a really thick cardboard. It takes forever to cut and just makes the whole process a thousand times more difficult than it needs to be.

Spray paint

I know that Krylon is a good brand of spray paint because people always ask about it and try to steal it. You can almost hear the sighs of disappointment when they discover that it's on the top shelf near the sales counter. Sucked in crims, we're onto you! I did ask one graffiti artist customer why Krylon is so sought after and apparently it's related to the coverage of the paint and the nozzle. Cheaper cans tend to have nozzles that clog more frequently and the spray doesn't cover as well, so you have to spend more time on the job. From my experience this is true. But of course that won't be an issue for you because you're not planning to decorate a train in five minutes before the cops arrive, are you?

SO, I'M NOT GOOD ENOUGH FOR YOU?

If you don't fancy coming up with your own stencil designs and think that the ideas for my projects are on the naff side, you can always trawl the net for some free downloadable ones. I've found that if you put the words 'free downloadable stencils spray' into a search engine you'll get heaps to choose from. If you just put in 'free downloadable stencils' you tend to get sites that offer a lot of rather twee decorative floral patterns, which lack the street cred you're probably looking for. Still, I suppose you could give the patterns a shot and just hope that people understand you're being ironic.

There are also acrylic sprays and enamel sprays. I've used both and found that enamel tends to cover a bit better than acrylic and is more readily available, so my advice to the beginner is to make your choice based on availability and color. Basically, just buy the one with the color that you're after. If you get into it you can get all picky, choosey and experimental with price, brand, nozzle and paint options.

I've also found that you can get some great metallic and fluorescent colors in auto centers. They're in the car touch-up sections and although the cans are smaller the colors can be unique.

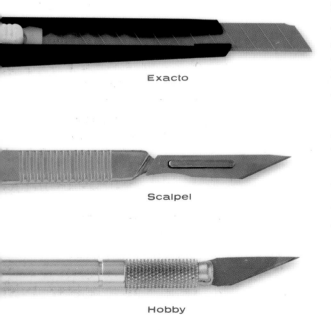

Exacto

Scalpel

Hobby

Blades

A hobby blade is a must here. By these I mean the ones with the round handle and the triangular blades that slide in at the top. You can get an actual scalpel if you want, but I think that's overkill. Believe it or not, they're the same scalpels surgeons wave over patients, which always creeps me out when I stop and think about it. Exacto knives, those ones with the flat snap-off blades, are good for cutting straight lines but not as great for curves and finer details. I say get the hobby knife with a protective cap for versatility. And pick up some spare blades while you're at it.

WARNING!!! As much as people scoff at stating the obvious, you do need to remember that blades are sharp and you do need to be careful with them. Hobby blades and scalpels are particularly lethal, much, much more so than the average kitchen knife (mine would be hard pressed to damage a tomato).

WARNING!!! As much as people scoff at stating the obvious, you do need to remember that **BLADES ARE SHARP** and you do need to be careful with them.

They're also smaller, so it's easier to jab or slice yourself accidentally. I've only damaged myself really badly when I was a cutting out stencils late at night and was rather tired. I let the tip of my finger hang over the ruler and ran the blade along the edge without thinking ... 5000 assorted swear words and thirty bandaids later I had learnt my lesson. So be careful with those blades, and if you've been cutting for while have a break so your concentration doesn't waiver.

It also goes without saying (but I'm going to say it) that you need to be super careful if you have kids around the place. Unsupervised blades and children together in the same room is a disaster waiting to happen. Do you really want to be the subject of a maimed kiddie newspaper story that will have readers rolling their eyes and wondering how you could be such an idiot?

Metal ruler

A metal ruler is a must as a guide and for cutting straight lines. A wooden or plastic one isn't good for this because running a blade along the edge tends to hack into those materials. There are usually two types of metal rulers, those with a rubber backing and those without. The rubber stops the ruler from sliding around when you run the blade along the edge. Personally, I use the ones without the rubber backing and I've never had any problems as long as I remember to press firmly on the ruler. However, if you are one of those people who aren't all that great at fiddly jobs go for the rubber-backed model. A standard 12" ruler is a good size to start with.

Photocopier

You don't have to have one of these next to your bed, but most people have access to one at work. If you make your design you can either draw or trace it onto stencil cardboard or you can use the photocopier. I'm big into the photocopying method because not only is it easier, but you can also use the photocopier controls to make the design larger or smaller. Although most of my stencil templates can be photocopied and cut out as is, I also give the percentages to use when increasing their size to Tabloid.

If you work in an office, all you have to do is stay back and photocopy your stencil onto cardboard when no one else is around. If you want to be really sneaky, you can always send an email regarding some work matter to your superior just before you leave. You can even mention it the next day so everyone thinks you were working back. It's true that you can't fool all the people all the time, but don't let that stop you from trying.

I DON'T HAVE ACCESS TO A PHOTOCOPIER SO HOW DO I GET THE DESIGNS ONTO THE CARDBOARD?

It may seem third world, but not everyone reading this book will have access to a photocopier. The following techniques work fine for designs that don't need to be enlarged:

● Trace over the design with tracing paper and a HB or 2B pencil. Flip the tracing paper over on to the stencil cardboard and scribble heavily over the lines. Remove the trace and you will find the lines of the design are on the card. You may need to touch them up a bit before cutting.

● Trace over the image with tracing paper and a pencil. Tape this to the back of your card and take it to the nearest window. You can see the design through the card so just trace over it again. Of course, don't lean heavily on the window and don't use a window with the sun shining directly into your eyes. Be sure the window is locked so you don't plunge to your death.

If you want to increase the size of designs without a photocopier then you'll just have to rely on your own drawing skills and try and reproduce deigns to the size you want. Sorry, but that's just the way it is.

SPRAY AND STAY SAFE

Spray paint on your canvas is a good thing, but spray paint in your lungs ain't quite so pretty. Always use some sort of mask when spraying and do so in a well-ventilated area, preferably outside. Although it is recommended that you use one of those respirator type masks that look like something from an old episode of *Dr Who*, I understand that that the majority of you probably won't do this because it's expensive and you're probably only doing one or two projects. At the very least wear a small white dust mask and remove yourself from the spraying area once you've finished. While it won't protect you from all the paint vapor, it will stop some getting through and also make you aware of the need to protect your respiratory bits. And don't pant like a dog while you're spraying either. I don't mean to sound like spray paint is going to kill you after one use, but I do want to alert you to possible dangers.

If you do decide to get right into stencil art and are spraying away for hours on end then you MUST purchase a full mask with at least two filters and use it every time you work. Gloves and eye protection are also mandatory. That paint doesn't only get into your body through your lungs, you know. If you think all this is uncool and unnecessary, then just picture the look on your grandchildren's faces when you breathe at them and sound like a vinyl lounge chair that's just been sat on. You can also look forward to a selection of nervous and circulatory problems to keep you company in your old age.

SPRAYING TECHNIQUE TIPS

- Shake the paint well before you spray. It says so right there on the can.

- Spray from a distance of about 4"–8". Any closer and you'll get big blobs of paint. Too far away and you won't get enough coverage.

- When you spray the can for the first time spray onto a piece of newspaper. Sometimes when you do the first spray the can may splutter the paint out leaving large blobs as opposed to a good, smooth finish. This doesn't happen all the time, but I say it's better to be safe before you've really started.

- Keep that can moving. Spend too long in one place and the paint will begin to pool into an uneven mass. Remember, a smooth, even finish is your goal.

- When you go to remove the stencil try to do so by lifting it from above, rather than dragging it off to the side. If the paint is still wet this can cause a dire case of smudging.

- Don't even think about stenciling if it's even a slightly windy day. The spray goes everywhere, the newspaper blows over onto the wet paint, the economy will go into decline and you'll find yourself attacked by werewolves. Okay, I'm getting carried away, but the fact is that it's just a big pain in the butt. Wait until it's relatively calm no matter how enthusiastic you are.

PROJECTS

I had a lot of fun coming up with these projects, but I think I had the most fun researching ideas. Often you can get so caught up on going from A to B that you fail to see the details. I found stencils in the oddest places—on mail boxes and tree stumps, all because I was looking. I hope that these projects make you more aware of the secret stenciling world, particularly if you live in an urban area. Just because it isn't nicely framed doesn't mean to say you can't stop, have a look and enjoy.

PROJECT 1

CD CIRCLES

With the advent of MP3s it seems that the once futuristic CD is fast becoming a quaint reminder of how we used to listen to music in the dark pre-internet ages. Like most people, I have a stack of music CDs I never use anymore. I attempted to sell mine to a hock shop but even they weren't all that interested, although they did buy a clock radio with a broken radio from the attractive lady in front of me. So rather than throw out the CDs I began to experiment only to find that they make a really good stencil, because they're flat, have some weight to them and are easy for most people to obtain.

Get this:

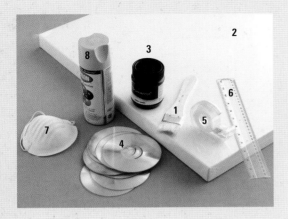

1. Medium sized flat brush

2. 24" x 24" pre-stretched canvas

3. 8 fl oz pot of burnt umber acrylic paint

4. 10 CDs that you don't want anymore

5. Adhesive tape

6. Ruler

7. Dust mask

8. Spray can of light beige enamel paint

Step 1

Put down plenty of newspaper. Using the flat brush paint the canvas with two coats of burnt umber acrylic paint. Allow it to dry between coats. Grab the CDs and place small pieces of adhesive tape over the holes in the center of each CD.

Step 3

Put the dust mask on and spray a generous coat of light beige spray paint over the entire surface. Leave the sides of the canvas alone — it creates a nice contrast when you hang this artwork on the wall. Keep spraying until you can't see the burnt umber base coat.

Step 2

Take the whole thing outside, and place it on a few sheets of newspaper. Arrange the CDs into a design you like. Use the main photograph on page 175 for guidance, and the ruler to ensure they are even.

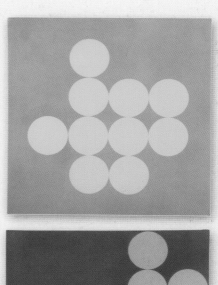

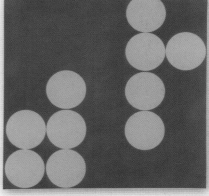

Step 4

Allow to dry before removing the CDs.

Variation I originally wanted this in bright retro colors. The above versions were my first choice. One day this book's photographer commented that "if the colors were more neutral I'd have this on my wall in a second." I have to admit he was right, it does look good— but just between you and me the purple and pink version is my big winner.

PROJECT 2

IT'S A BIRD! IT'S A PLANE! NO, IT'S A PLANE!

There's nothing like the sound of birds flying over the rooftops, particularly when that bird is actually a screaming airplane and you're trying to have a conversation with your friend while watching TV. This project continues my interest in urban landscapes and is one of my favorites in this book.

It's also an example of combining techniques. We are going to use stenciling and markers to get this one together. Although I have presented these sections as separate chapters that doesn't mean you have to be strict about using them separately. Take the technique of one project and add it to another if you want. You never know, it just might turn out to be the best thing you've ever done, and you wouldn't want to miss out on that, would you?

Get this:

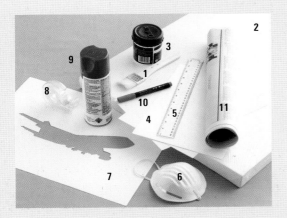

1. Medium sized flat brush

2. 20" x 30" pre-stretched canvas

3. 8 fl oz tester pot of sky blue acrylic paint

4. 3 x Letter sheets of cardboard

5. Ruler

6. Dust mask

7. Tabloid size cut out airplane stencil
   (See Templates, page 218)

8. Sticky tape

9. Dark red spray paint

10. Red medium sized bullet point permanent marker

11. Newspaper

Step 1

Put down plenty of newspaper. Using the flat brush, paint the canvas with two coats of sky blue paint. Allow it to dry between coats. Take the canvas outside and put down more newspaper. Place the three cardboard sheets at angles so they form the rooftop shapes. Tuck a sheet of newspaper under the cardboard to protect the rest of the canvas. Put the dusk mask on, shake that can of red spray paint and apply a good coat. Allow to dry before removing the cardboard.

Step 4

Spray an even coat of the red enamel paint over the airplane stencil. Allow to dry before removing the stencil.

Step 2

Position your airplane stencil near the top of the canvas.

Step 3

Now get a few sheets of newspaper and tape them to the stencil edges so that the remainder of the canvas is covered. We are doing this to shield the canvas from the spray paint, otherwise you'll get a faint border appearing around the edges of your stencil.

Step 5

Use the red permanent marker and ruler to draw three or so antennas. Just use the ones in my example as a guide, or go and look at some next time you're wandering around the street.

Beware! I know all this business of sticking pieces of paper onto the stencil seems really annoying, but if you look closely above you'll see an oblong of spray paint around the plane—so, you can see why it's worth the effort.

PROJECT 3

ARCADE GAME

Video game graphics are so realistic now that it's hard to imagine that games like *Galaxian* and *Space Invaders* were considered pretty "out there" in their day. Although I'm all for the new graphic technology, I still have a soft spot for these older graphics, and their squared-off shapes are perfect for stenciling. Although this is a multi-canvas project, all the canvases are rather small, and the whole process shouldn't take longer than a couple of hours, max. So set aside some time and before you know it, today's high score winner in the art arcade games could be you! (You know, I've really got to do something about saying uncool things like that.)

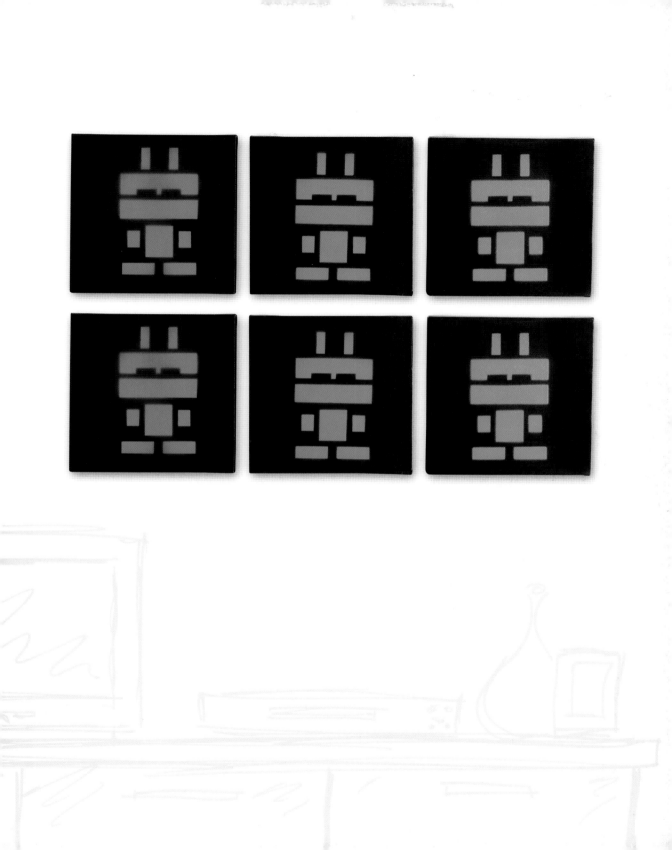

Get this:

1. Medium sized flat brush

2. Six 10" x 10" pre-stretched canvases

3. Tabloid size cut out alien stencil (See Templates, page 218)

4. Lime green enamel spray paint

5. Dust mask

6. 8 fl oz pot of ivory black acrylic paint

Step 1

Put plenty of newspaper down. Using the flat brush paint the canvas with two coats of ivory black paint. Allow it to dry between coats.

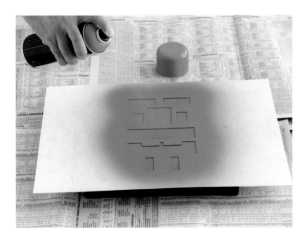

Step 3

Spray a good coat of lime green enamel paint, with the dust mask on of course. Allow to dry before removing the stencil.

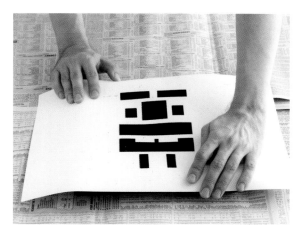

Step 2

Go outside and place the Tabloid alien stencil on the canvas and ensure that the alien design is somewhere in the middle. Put a heap of newspaper under the lot.

Step 4

Repeat this process on the remaining five canvases. Leave around 10–20 minutes between canvases so the stencil has time to dry and doesn't smudge paint everywhere. Don't worry if all your aliens aren't in the same spot each time — mine aren't. It adds a little bit of movement to the final group.

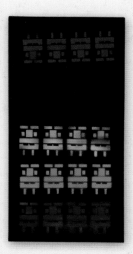

In the beginning: I just thought I'd show you how this project initially started out. I decided not to use it because the alien quartet stencil takes a while to cut out and I didn't want to put any beginners off. It takes too long to make because you have to allow for each alien row to dry before moving onto the next.

TIP

■ The stencil design for this project is composed of straight lines. If you're new to the whole stencil cutting business, use a metal ruler to guide your hobby blade — it makes the job quicker and easier.

PROJECT 4

OLD SCHOOL SKULL

This project wasn't always called old school skull. I showed an early prototype to a very young skater artist who comes into the shop and he said: "Yeah I like it. I'm into old school." While I didn't think it was cutting edge or anything I also didn't think that it was so outdated that it had actually become somewhat cool again. I suppose we all reach a point where something we like is seen as old school by someone who is part of the new school. Sigh. But old school or not, I'm up to my usual tricks again and I am pushing the concept of combining techniques, in this case collage and spray stenciling. I've said it once (I think) and I'll say it again—any of the techniques in this book can be combined. Don't be afraid that you'll do something wrong or make a mistake, and certainly don't let your fear of not doing something that looks like my final picture stop you from trying. Not doing something because you think you might fail? Now if you ask me, that's old school. And saying corny things like that is pretty old school as well.

Get this:

1. Scissors

2. Newspaper

3. 10" x 10" pre-stretched canvas

4. Medium sized flat brush

5. Binder medium

6. Yellow enamel spray paint

7. Dust mask

8. Tabloid size cut out skull stencil (See Templates, page 219)

9. Black enamel spray paint

Step 1

Using the scissors, trim a sheet of newspaper to just slightly larger than your canvas, ensuring that you will have enough to cover the sides. Using the flat brush, paint the canvas (including the sides) with a coat of binder medium.

Step 3

Take the artwork outside and put down more newspaper. Spray a few random curved lines on the front with the yellow spray paint. Allow it to dry. Cover your mouth with the dust mask while spraying, of course.

Step 2

Quickly place the sheet of newspaper onto the front of the canvas and stick it down over the sides, trimming the corners and any stray bits with the scissors. If it looks a bit rough don't worry. Street art looks better this way. Allow it to dry.

Variation Although I've used newspaper as my background, you can pretty much use anything. Here are some examples so you can see what I mean. The red roses one is wrapping paper and the orange one uses corrugated cardboard from a carton.

Step 4

Position your skull stencil on the front of the canvas. It doesn't have to be centered. Put the mask on again and apply a coat of black enamel spray paint and allow to dry before removing the stencil.

TIPS

- When you stick the newspaper onto the canvas the water in the binder medium can cause the paper to buckle and bubble. Don't go nuts trying to fix it. Just leave it alone until it dries and you'll find that the buckles practically go away, or at least reduce in size.

- If you do use newspaper, like I have, for your background then make sure the piece you select doesn't have large type or images on it, because when you spray the skull onto the paper it can get lost in the background.

PROJECT 5

SOFT STENCIL

Although stenciling has a reputation for being hard-edged and very graphic, there are ways to soften the look and give the appearance of texture as opposed to hard lines. I was at home in the country when I came a across an old fabric store carrying stock that had its heyday with German prostitutes in the mid-eighties. Among the bolts I found a white polyester lace that actually made me break out into a rash just looking at it. I immediately bought a few yards from a woman who gave me some rather odd looks (Hey, it's for a stenciling! No really it is!) and went home to experiment. I loved the final result, but something was missing and I couldn't quite figure it out. The solution came to me the next morning. This is one of the projects that looks good alone, but even better as part of a pair. I can't explain it but some paintings, like some people, just work better with a partner.

Get this:

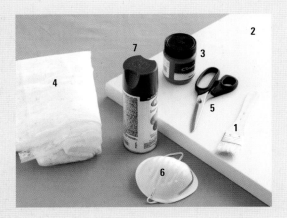

1. Medium sized flat brush

2. 20" x 24" pre-stretched canvas

3. 8 fl oz pot of cadmium red hue acrylic paint

4. A yard of lacy polyester material

5. Scissors

6. Dust mask

7. Spray can of blue enamel paint

Step 1

Using the flat brush, paint the canvas with two coats of red acrylic paint. Allow it to dry between coats. Now go outside and put down lots of newspaper. Cut a length of the lace fabric using the scissors.

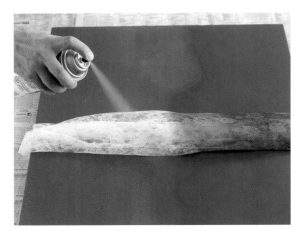

Step 3

Get that dust mask on and spray an even coat of blue enamel paint over the whole canvas, including the lace-wrapped section. Allow it to dry.

Step 2

Take the canvas outside and put it on a few sheets of newspaper. Scrunch and roll the fabric into a sausage shape and tuck it under both sides of the canvas as shown above.

Step 4

Remove the lace and see what your design has turned out like. Happy? Excellent—do another one so you can put them side by side. Unhappy? Never mind, just wait until the spray is dry then repeat all of the previous steps again until you're beaming at the result.

TIPS

■ I did explore the possibility of using the lace flat but I found it produced something that looked more aunty that arty. Experiment yourself and see if you get the same vibe.

■ Try to scrunch and fold the lace loosely so you get a variation in the amount of paint that passes through the fabric.

■ I like the idea of leaving the sides of this canvas the original red color rather than spraying them blue as well. Looks interesting when hung on the wall.

■ Wear that bloody dust mask—you know you should.

PROJECT 6

NEGATIVE STENCIL

A woman came into the shop last weekend and wanted to know if we knew of anyone who printed large photos on plastic. We couldn't help her, but it did get me thinking about how fascinated I used to be with the negatives in our old family photo box. I loved to hold them up to the light and see a world with white trees, black skies and people with black teeth. That's what inspired me to come up with a project that allows you to create your very own negative style artwork. That and the fact that I would have to sell my left kidney if I actually wanted to get something professionally printed on plastic. You would not believe how much it costs. The unusual thing about this piece of artwork is that because it's transparent you get the color of your walls showing through. You also get the play of light and shadow on the design because it sits out from the stretcher frame. I didn't find this out until I had this piece on the wall for a few hours. See, even I'm learning things as we go along.

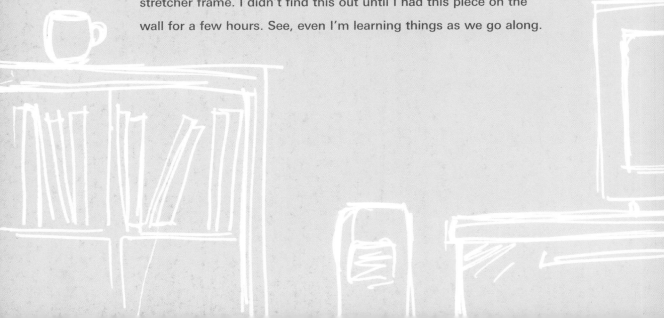

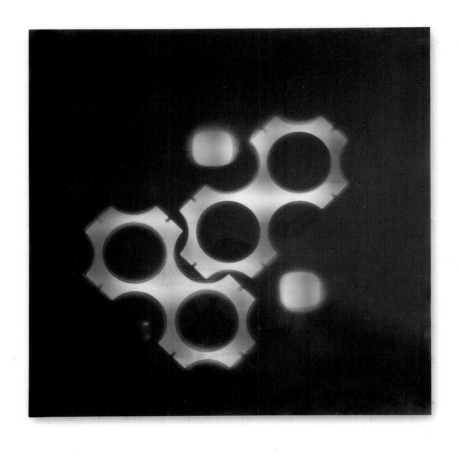

Get this:

1. 20" x 20" pre-stretched canvas

2. 234" x 331" thick acetate sheet

3. Scissors

4. Tube of black acrylic paint

5. Black medium sized bullet tip permanent marker

6. Takeout container lid

7. Can of black spray enamel paint

8. Exacto knife

9. Roll of double-sided adhesive tape

10. Plastic shapes/kitchen utensils (shape items)

11. Dust mask

12. Medium sized flat brush

Step 1

Place the canvas on a corner of the acetate sheet about ½" in from the side and the bottom, and trace around it with the black permanent marker. Use the scissors to cut out the square shape. We want the acetate to be slightly larger than the frame so that no frame will be showing on the final artwork.

Step 4

Get that dust mask on and spray several light coats of paint until you can't see the newspaper through the acetate. Leave everything alone until the paint is dry—about 20 minutes. While waiting, squeeze out some black paint onto the container lid. Using the flat brush paint the sides of the canvas. Leave to dry. Remove the shape items from the now dry acetate sheet.

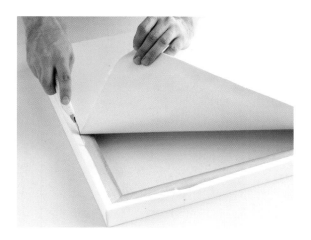

Step 2

Use the exacto knife to cut the canvas out of the frame.

Step 3

Put down heaps of newspaper — outdoors of course — then place the acetate down and the frame on top of that. Arrange your shape items inside the stretcher bar frame then remove the frame leaving the objects where they are. We are doing this to ensure that the design falls within the borders of the stretcher frame. Try not to place your shape items all at the top of the acetate so that if you decide to place a hanging system on the back it won't be too visible — see Chapter 12 for more information on this.

Step 5

Flip the canvas frame over so the flat edge is facing you. Place two rows of double-sided adhesive across the top section of the stretcher frame, then position the painted side of the acetate sheet on the adhesive.

TIP

■ I got my shape items from a second-hand store and my kitchen. I used an old plastic wine rack and a couple of empty yogurt pots, but you can use anything that's solid and unwanted. Think coathangers, jars, old kitchen utensils. Metal and mechanical spare parts almost always have interesting shapes.

Well hung:

(sorry, I couldn't help myself)

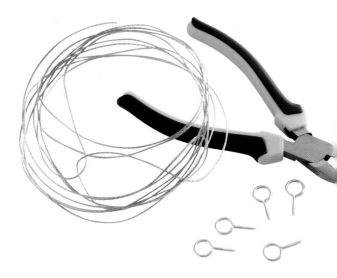

Are you one of those people who thinks you need a fishing line to hang a picture? When a customer asks for fishing line I always know it's got nothing to do with Nemo and everything to do with hanging something on their walls. I don't know where this urban myth started but I can assure you it's not the best thing to use. Fishing line is far too slippery and fiddly to use. Have you ever tried to tie a good knot with it? But don't panic because there is a solution. It's called hanging wire (also known as picture wire), and it's available from both hardware and art stores.

Hanging wire comes in different thicknesses and (funnily enough) looks like string made of wire. However, it's much stronger than string, which can deteriorate over time—and when you least expect it—the string snaps and your picture goes into free fall. I love art but I certainly don't want to wake up with a canvas sitting on my face in the middle of the night, although I'm sure there's a website out there dedicated to folks who do.

Firstly, you need to determine if you even need a hanging system for your picture. Some pictures can just fit over a nail or hook in the wall if it extends far enough. It's not ideal, but I have pictures on my wall hung this way and they seem to be doing fine. The only problem is that they tend to blow off the wall if I leave the side door open on a windy day. And don't forget that not all pictures actually need to be on a wall. Some can look quite at home sitting on a mantelpiece or credenza. (A credenza is a fancy name for one of those low standing long cupboards. I thought I'd use that word because I only found out what it meant two weeks ago when an interior designer explained it to me very s-l-o-w-l-y, with a smug expression on her face. Honestly, some people.) I have also seen people just lean large pictures against the wall, but unless the picture is absolutely monstrous I always think it looks as if they've just moved in and haven't sorted things out yet. However, if you live in a gothic mansion and have paintings that stretch to the ceiling then I'd say give it a go.

On the whole, practically all medium-to-large stretch canvases need some sort of hanging system. A simple way to do this is to buy a small picture-hanging kit from a hardware store. These usually consist of four screw eyes and a length of hanging wire in a little pack. These are generally only suitable for lighter pictures. If you have a larger/heavier canvas you will need larger and stronger screw eyes. You will also have to look at a thicker grade of hanging wire than the type that comes in the little packets I just mentioned.

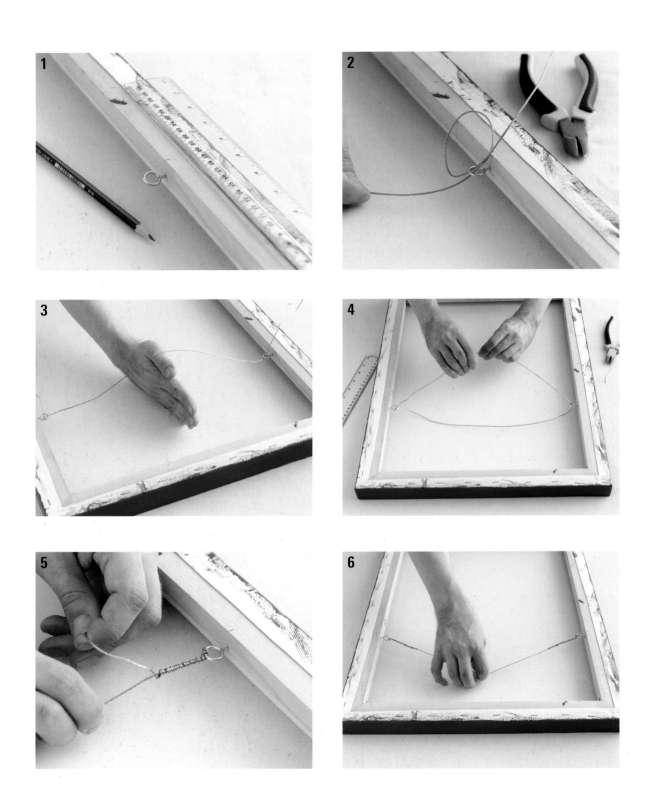

You will also need some sort of snips to cut the wire. Scissors will work for really thin hanging wires, but thicker versions need something sturdier. I use a pair of small cutting pliers that I bought from a hardware store. If you do decide to use your scissors with the thick stuff then do so with the understanding that they'll probably never work properly again, and even if they do the cutting blades will be blunt and distorted beyond belief. Don't say I didn't warn you.

BECOMING WELL HUNG—THE G-RATED VERSION

1. Insert the screw eyes about one third of the way down. This is a good spot because if you go too low the painting will lean too far forward from the wall. Any higher and the hanging wire could show above the artwork and that only looks good in houses owned by people who smell like mothballs. The wood in pre-stretched canvases is usually pretty soft, so just push the screw eyes in and start turning. If you're having trouble, then use a hammer and nail or drill to make a small hole to get things started. Place the screw eyes on the inside of the wooden stretcher frame, so they don't stick out and damage your wall. Use a ruler to make sure both screw eyes are directly across from each other.

2. Pass a length of wire through each of the screw eyes, then loop the wire again.

3. The wire needs to be slightly loose so don't loop it like you're stringing a guitar—it puts too much stress on the wire when you suspend it from the nail or hook. As a general rule, you should be able to fit your hand, karate-chop-style, under the wire. Keep it reasonably loose but not so loose that it hangs above the picture. Remember what I said about mothballs.

4. Leave about 6–8" spare at either side.

5. Twist the excess wire tightly back over the section within the screw eyes as per the picture. Notice I said twist not knot. A knot doesn't work as well with hanging wire as the twisting does and you do want things to be as secure as possible. Just keep twisting until there's nothing left to twist.

6. The completed version should look something like this. If you can't get hold of hanging wire then try to use a thinnish nylon cord. Just loop it through the screw eyes and tie a knot. You can also tie knots at the ends to stop the cord from fraying or slipping. I've found nylon cord is less prone to deterioration than your average piece of string.

You may also have noticed that some galleries have these very slick rail and suspension systems for hanging their artwork. It's normally a rail high on the wall with a series of clear strings that hang down with adjustable hooks for the pictures to hang on. Most art stores don't sell these so if this is the sort of system you're after you will have to trawl the net and find a framing specialist who does.

Some of you may be wondering just what nails and hooks should go into your walls. My rule is that if it's wood then hammer a nail in and if it's cement or plaster then drill and fill it with a hook or nail and one of those plastic thingos that stop the plaster from crumbling. Sorry folks, but any questions about your wall and hook combinations are going to have to be answered by your local hardware store. After all my father once described me as 'someone who thinks manual labor is a Spanish matador.'

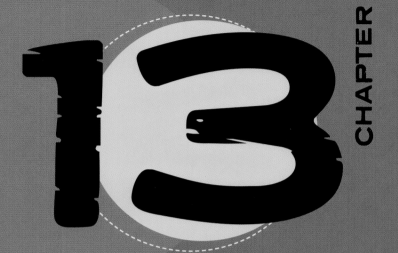

Art galleries

I really like going to art galleries; big or small, I always try to check one out every week. They can be intimidating at first, but don't let that stop you from stepping in the door. It's not like expensive stores where the staff can give you that "buy or get out" attitude. Smaller art galleries exist so people can have a look, so you'll often find the staff are generally friendly in a reserved sort of way and basically leave you alone to wander at your leisure. And the major public art institutions are pretty much the same, except that there is usually a café where you can get a good coffee and a nice sweetie when you feel like a break.

Major art institutions are usually government funded and hold exhibitions from local or overseas artists. The works aren't for sale, and revenue is raised by charging admission fees, memberships, subscriptions, and the like. By contrast, the smaller commercial galleries are privately owned and run to make a profit by selling the work on display.

I used to wonder how artworks ended up in smaller galleries. This usually happens one of two ways:

1) The owners find the artists themselves through their own connections.

2) They accept submissions from potential candidates who can either be established or emerging artists, then sort through them to see what they think will work best (i.e. sell) in their gallery.

There are also two types of smaller commercial galleries; privately-run galleries and artist-run galleries.

As I said, privately-run galleries accept submissions from, or seek out, artists whose art they think will work in their gallery. Once they agree to take an artist on, the gallery pays the printing costs for the invitations, any alcohol on opening night and associated exhibition costs. They also have a mailing list of potential clients who may be interested in the work. One big advantage of a privately run gallery is that they often keep examples of artists' work in their storerooms after the exhibition is over so a client can come in and see/buy work from the stockroom stash. In return for all this the owner receives a cut of the profits on each sale, which is usually in the 30–40 percent range.

Artist-run galleries and spaces are somewhat less structured. Artists usually have to send a submission to have an exhibition, and are expected to pay for the rental of the gallery during their allotted time. They also have to look after the place during opening hours. The artist often has to cover the costs of printing the invitations and any booze and snacks on opening night. Bear in mind that this could prove fatal to your budget, particularly if your circle of friends includes some highly seasoned boozebags like mine. No pre-existing client lists exist so artists have to do their own publicity and sort out whom they would like to invite. The owners sometimes receive a commission from any sales, but one of the big advantages is that they are generally more open to new and emerging artists. It's not unusual for artists to begin their careers with exhibitions in these type of galleries.

ART GALLERY EXHIBITIONS—I'M HERE FOR THE ART BUT WHERE'S THE BAR?

Artist run or privately owned, big or small, underground or mainstream, one thing all galleries have in common is opening nights for exhibitions. This is where some lucky artist gets to invite a whole heap of buddies and buyers to see his/her latest collection of artworks.

The one thing you will notice when you go to an art exhibition opening is that there tends to be a large gathering of patrons in one area. Are they looking at some amazing piece of art? Are they witnessing a new technique that will set off a new art movement? Are they enthralled by the beauty of the artist's subject?

No, they're waiting for a drink.

Although the bar is certainly a popular place to be, most attendees will also wander around and gather in groups to discuss the work on the walls, so free booze isn't the only drawcard, although it certainly seems to be for some.

ART CRASHER

With smaller galleries you generally don't need to pay to go to an exhibition opening nor do you need to be personally invited. You certainly don't need a ticket—just show up and wander in. Sometimes you may have to pay for the drinks but generally they're on the house. Still, if you're not sure just ring up the gallery and ask. I'm sure they won't mind.

HOW DO I FIND OUT ABOUT EXHIBITIONS?

Major art shows are regularly advertised in newspapers and on street banners. Although the smaller ones can't afford that sort of publicity, they still manage to get a mention in the arts sections and exhibition listings of broadsheet newspapers.

Another source of information is, of course, your local art store. Most will have exhibition cards posted on a noticeboard or in the window. These tell you the artist, the gallery details and the dates and times for the opening night. Anyone can usually attend these so feel free to drop in.

Even if you don't live in a city, most places have their regional art galleries, which are always worth a look. Ask at your local tourist center and they'll probably give you a list of places you didn't even know existed. Local colleges and schools also have final year shows open to the public. I know it doesn't sound as glamorous as some ritzy urban art gallery affair but that doesn't mean you can't appreciate what's on offer. You might even pick up some ideas to use yourself. Everyone has to start somewhere, and that includes exhibitors and attendees.

If you work in the CBD of a major city it's likely that there will be some exhibitions within walking distance. They can be found in libraries or sometimes even department stores. Pack your lunch and make the effort to wander around these exhibitions. No point spending every lunch hour eating at your desk and playing on Facebook.

ART EXHIBITION OPENING NIGHTS

I really like going to opening nights, particularly if I know the artist. It's good to see their work and I feel I've done my duty in supporting them. (Not that it's a duty of course, but you know what I mean.) It's also a chance to catch up with other friends and have a drink at the local pub afterwards. I also like to see the galleries themselves; some are in the most amazing buildings and parts of the city that I haven't been to before, and the interiors can be more interesting than what's on the walls. Sometimes you even see the odd famous person, which always gives that star-struck bumpkin country hick part of me a minor thrill.

Although it may seem that art exhibition openings are reserved for an arty few, that's not the case. Granted, not all major art galleries have an open door policy on opening nights, but a lot of the smaller ones do. They're usually held from 6 pm to 8 pm weeknights so you can be home tucked up in bed at a respectable hour if need be. Although there's booze, there's usually no food at all so you may have to sneak out and wolf down a chocolate bar from a convenience store at some point.

When you arrive, be sure to look for one of the room sheets, which are usually located near the entrance. Basically this is just a sheet with a listing of the works, their numbers, titles and prices. If you are new to the exhibition scene a room sheet can help you navigate your way around if there are a few areas to check out. Just start at number one and keep on movin'.

I have been to a few opening nights on my own, but I always feel slightly awkward. I'm not the type to make protracted conversations with strangers, so I usually just do a scan of the artwork before making my way home. I always feel much better if I'm going with a friend or plan to meet someone there, and unless you've got loads of confidence I suggest you do the same. I don't know about you, but I always feel like some sort of lost ghost wandering around while everyone else is chatting away.

While most independent galleries are happy for anyone to rock up, larger galleries will usually issue invitations for some of their more prestigious openings. If these interest you, inquire at the information desk or online about becoming a gallery member or buying some sort of yearly subscription. Member benefits frequently include previews and invites to certain exhibitions so you get to support the arts and booze it up at several exclusive events. Now that's what I call a win-win situation.

WHAT DO I WEAR?

I always roll my eyes in movies where they show an art exhibition opening with loads of skinny people dressed in avant-garde black clothes swanning around and talking about "existentialist this" and "juxtaposition that." Although I'm sure some exhibitions are like that, I've never been to one, and I've been to a lot. The reality is that you can wear almost anything. There's usually a good lot of people in street wear, a few fashionably dressed vintage clothing types, some middle-aged women in purple and a sprinkling of people fresh from work and still in their suits. There really is no dress code at all. I've gone to many straight from work in the most casual of clothes and no one seemed to care. I've even worn shorts and my linty pins certainly aren't anything to write home about. The moral of the story is to wear what you like (but if you're really not sure then dress down).

EXHIBITION FAUX PAS—ARE YOU GUILTY?

● Don't dis the paintings too loudly. The artist might be standing close by and doesn't really want to know that your eight-year-old niece could do a better job. Besides that, it's just plain rude.

● If you know the artist congratulate them—even if you hate the work. A lot of effort goes into these things. I once attended an exhibition by two girls that was so bad I admired them for having the guts to actually show up at all. Maybe that's why they were stoned off their chops that night. However, I still did my bit and wished them all the best. Sometimes you just gotta do what you gotta do.

● If you know the artist make the effort to turn up on their opening night. Opening nights are like parties—head count makes a big difference. They really will appreciate you being there even if you only chat to each other for a few minutes.

● If you are interested in buying something but are not sure who to speak to then ask at the bar. They are usually connected to the gallery manager in some way and can help you out.

● Had such a good time you want to come back again? Ask to have your name added to the gallery mailing list, that way you'll get invitations to openings and updates sent directly to you.

What Do The Dots Mean?

A red dot means that the painting has been sold and the artist will be smiling. A half-red dot means that a buyer has expressed a strong interest in an artwork and it has been sort of reserved. The artist will still be smiling—maybe a half smile? Some galleries also use black dots instead of red, with some waffle that it doesn't detract from the artwork in the way red can. It means the same thing so I think they're just being trendy.

Even though the artwork has been sold it's not like you're at the supermarket and you take your goods with you immediately after the sale. It stays in the gallery until the actual exhibition is over.

Real life weekend artist—profile 2

Jason Young is also another regular in the art store. What I remember most about him is that he was always asking questions about products; what is this? What will that do? What will happen if I mix this with that? After a while he became one of the store regulars and I would see him and his girlfriend walking their dog around where I live. We got chatting in the store and I was surprised to find that he also had a full-time job, as he bought so many things I assumed he spent most of his time painting.

Did you study art at all?

No, I studied accountancy and now I work as a mortgage broker and in property sales.

So how did you go from mortgage broker to artist?

I had a friend in New York who was an artist. I would visit him for a few weeks every year and help out in his studio. It was a lot of fun and gave me some idea of how to go from A to B with a canvas. Painting is one of those things I'd always planned on doing later in life, but one day I just decided that I needed a creative outlet from my regular job. I literally went to the art store bought a stack of materials and just started painting. I had neither the time nor the inclination to go back to university to study art. I felt working full-time was a good thing because I had the money to buy materials and experiment. I found that my friend in New York who was pursuing art full-time never had any money to buy materials, so whenever he had some he would try and hit a home run for fear of wasting materials. My philosophy was to buy materials, start, experiment, discard what didn't work and start again, and my full-time wage made this a possibility.

How did you start going commercial?

The usual way: by doing things for friends and family. After three years I had my own show at an artist-run space that was popular with art students who gave me a lot of critical feedback. I also wanted to see if this was just a hobby or if I wanted to take it seriously. I sold half a dozen artworks.

I have no faith in medicine 2005

Drought 2005

Misty waters 2004

What do you mostly work in?

Mixed media, tending towards oils, but I use a broad range of materials from art store purchases to house paint and enamels.

When do you paint?

Before this year I had a more flexible schedule and basically painted whenever I felt like it. I've recently gone back into an office environment and so I haven't painted for a couple of months, but I'm looking to get back into it again. I have tried to box my creative time into a schedule but that doesn't work for me because I may feel like painting at night or doing something quickly before I go to work.

What's your inspiration?

Trying to come up with something new. Nothing bores me more than something that is too directly related to the work of another artist. I respect artists who try to push the boundaries. I think you should experiment with materials. Just have a go. Because I've never studied art I don't have any defined boundaries of what's right and what's wrong when it comes to what you can do with materials. I like to see how far I can push things and just see what happens when you mix this with that or do this with that.

14

Getting your art out there

Although having work in an art gallery is a good ego stroker, you do have to be a more established artist for your applications to be successful. But don't despair; there are other avenues to explore if you really want to get your art out there. Consider the following:

SMALL GIFT AND INTERIOR STORES

Many of these types of stores are interested in stocking exclusive decor items that aren't available in larger chains. Although you might be brimming with enthusiasm, don't just barrel in there with a sackful of paintings like some mad person on day release. Ring and speak to the manager. Sound them out and see if they are into the idea before making an appointment to show them a few pieces. I've actually done this myself and I think you'll be surprised just how many people are willing to see what you have to offer. I'd also advise you to start small; most stores are willing to go with some small to medium sized pieces as opposed to some gigantic monster painting that costs a fortune. And be sure to keep the prices in line with the other things they sell. The owner will also expect a cut, so negotiate prices that will keep you both happy.

This worked quite well for me and the only real problem I had was remembering just what paintings were in what store. Don't be a dope like me—keep records to avoid this problem.

CAFES

Many cafés display paintings for sale. You might like to inquire if they would like to display yours. Cafés do get an enormous amount of human traffic and that sort of exposure can only be a good thing. It's also satisfying just to go to said café with a friend and modestly point out just whose paintings are on the wall.

CERTAIN PUBS

Not all pubs have art on their walls for sale but I have noticed some of them do. This is a tricky one because most people in pubs aren't there for the paintings and I'm not sure the staff would be willing to guard your artwork with their lives if the brawl to end all brawls broke out unexpectedly. I've never done this myself and I'm not sure if this avenue is worth exploring, but I've included it because it just might be the thing for someone out there. I did go and see a band in a pub last weekend and there were some pieces on the wall behind the bar but it was one of those places where I felt I should be asking the barman for ID. Maybe this one is best left to young urban-hipster types.

It **DOESN'T MATTER** if it's good taste, it doesn't matter if it's **BAD** taste. Just so long as it's **YOUR TASTE.**

MARKET STALLS

If you're somewhat prolific in your painting you can always hire a stall at your local market and see how you go. Once again, have a range of prices and sizes. People who impulse buy want to be able to carry things around with them. Markets are all over the place in major cities, and rural centers are in on the act as well, so the best places to find out about them are your local tourist information center. I'd also recommend that you have some sort of business card available as well. Some people like to consider things before they buy them (I'm one of this breed) and you want them to be able to contact you easily if they decide to purchase. I'd also recommend you bring your thickest skin. I've done the markets thing and it's not uncommon for shoppers to openly critique what's on display to their friends. Sometimes it's good and sometimes you'll wonder just how some people were brought up. Sorry, but you'll just have to bite your tongue when you know they should be watching theirs. Console yourself with the fact that at least you're out there doing your thing. How many people can honestly say that?

It also helps to do this with a friend. That way you have someone to help you set up and to chat with. Things can get pretty slow if it's a quiet day. If you can't get someone for the whole day consider getting someone to drop by while you have a break and get some lunch. Good friends and family will be hopefully impressed enough to help you out on this one. If there's no takers then bring a book and lunch and ask a stall neighbor to keep an eye on things if you have to go somewhere. Unless they've got a bladder of steel you'll probably find yourself returning the favor at some point during the day.

If you decide to go the markets route try to do it a few times on a regular basis so people start to see your work. It will also show you just how much sales can vary depending on the date. In addition, you'll get an idea of the sizes and styles that are most popular.

FAMILY, FRIENDS, AND FRIENDS OF FRIENDS

It's great when someone likes what you do so much that they want you to do something for them. By all means take the job on, but make sure you charge a reasonable price that covers the cost of materials and your time. Agree on this before you start, otherwise you'll end up charging less than you should. Still, that's not always a bad thing. Sometimes when you start out just the sheer excitement of seeing your paintings on any wall apart from your own is all the payment you need. It's not uncommon for people to undercharge at the beginning. Just make sure that things don't stay that way.

THE STORE WILL BE CLOSING IN
TEN MINUTES ...

Well, it looks like it's time to go, so I'll wrap this up now with a little true story that got me started on this whole idea.

A customer came into the store. He had a few bare walls, money to burn, and thought that he needed something to decorate his new house. Half an hour later he left with a few canvases, a bit of paint, and a few ideas from me. A couple of months went by and he returned to buy more art supplies. He said that he was going to make a few more paintings until he could find something decent to replace them with. I asked him if he was happy with his artistic efforts. Yes, he was. Did he enjoy doing them? Very much so. Did his friends like them? Yes, they all did. The bottom line was he felt that his work wasn't that of a real artist.

He never came in again and I sometimes wonder if he did actually get around to buying "something decent" to replace his own art with. And if he did replace them, I hope he didn't replace them all. While it's great to buy the creativity of a real artist, it's just as nice, maybe even nicer, to show off a bit of your own.

Templates

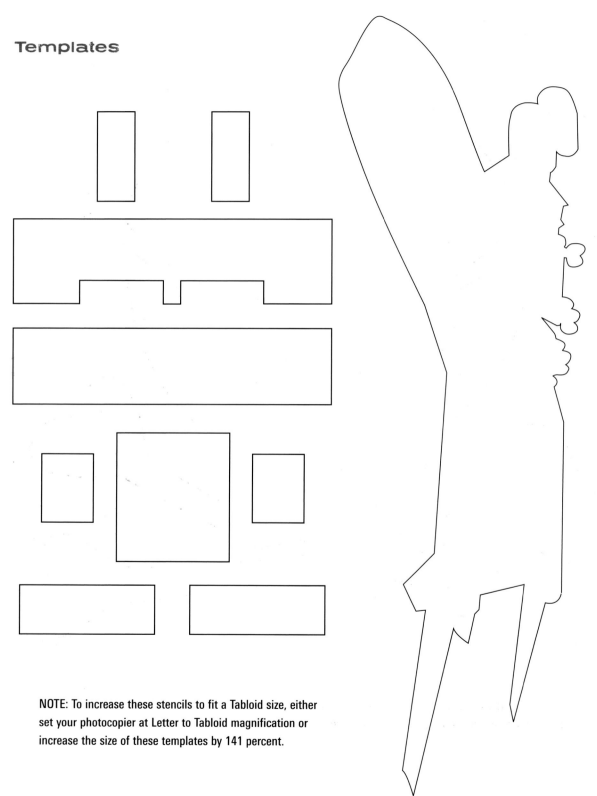

NOTE: To increase these stencils to fit a Tabloid size, either set your photocopier at Letter to Tabloid magnification or increase the size of these templates by 141 percent.

NOTE: This stencil does not need to be increased in size.
Simply photocopy on to Tabloid card at 100 percent.

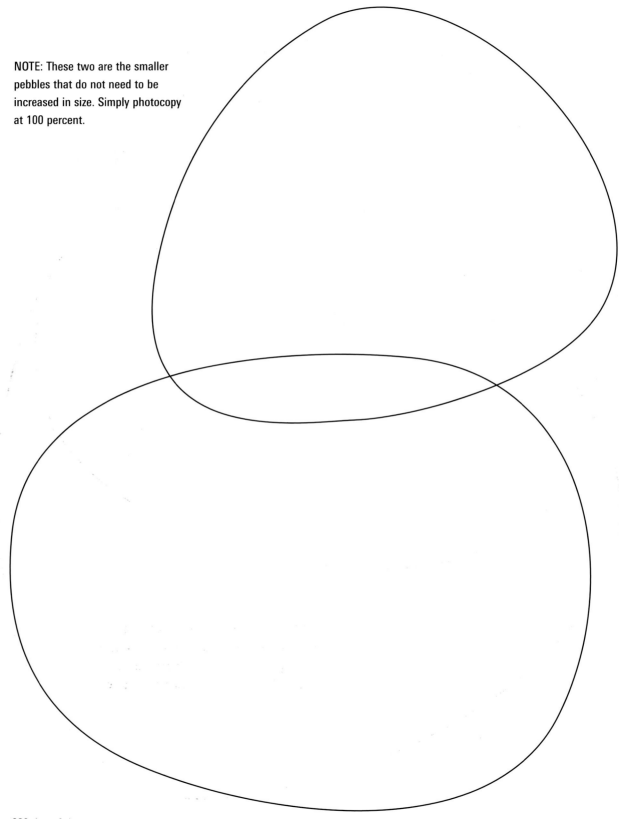

NOTE: These two are the smaller pebbles that do not need to be increased in size. Simply photocopy at 100 percent.

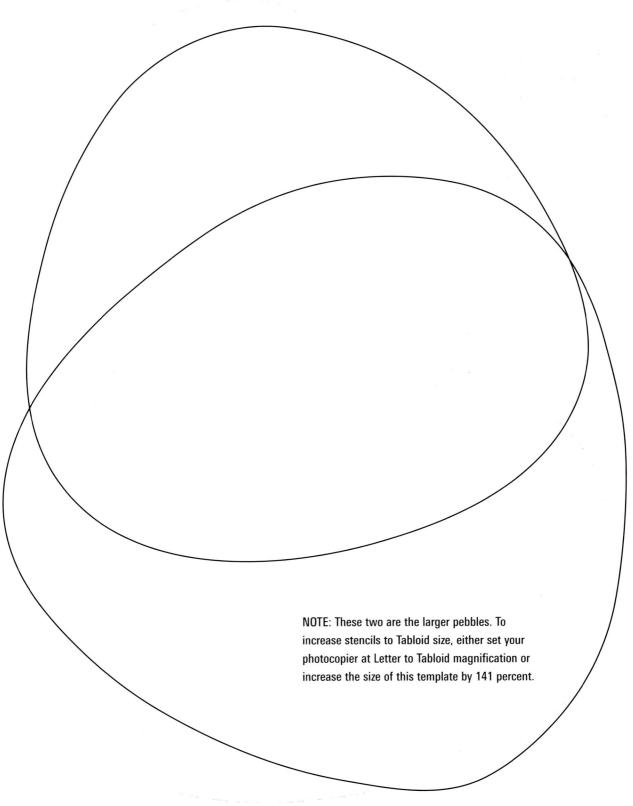

NOTE: These two are the larger pebbles. To increase stencils to Tabloid size, either set your photocopier at Letter to Tabloid magnification or increase the size of this template by 141 percent.

CANVAS SIZE: 36″ x 24″

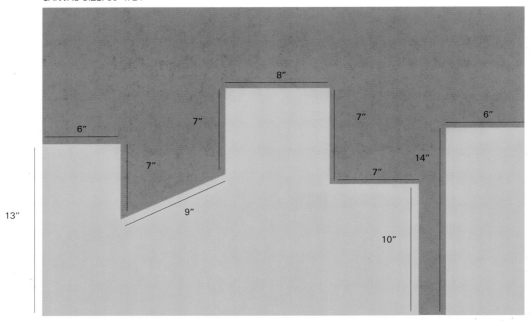

CANVAS SIZE: 36″ x 48″

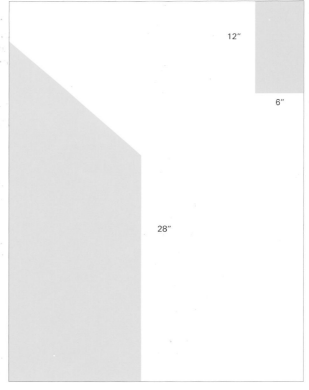

index